Published by MANAS-SYSTEMS
Post Office Box 5153, Fullerton, CA 92635
Copyright© 1982, Keith Golay

Distributed by Keigh Golay, Ph.D. & Associates
100 West Valencia Mesa Drive, Suite 203
Fullerton, CA 92635 (714) 870-4355

Fifth Printing

ISBN: 0-9610076-0-5
Library of Congress Catalog Card Number 82-62144

Learning Patterns
and
Temperament Styles

by

Keith Golay, Ph.D.

Published by MANAS-SYSTEMS

Table of Contents

Acknowledgements

I first want to thank David Keirsey, whom I consider to be my most influential teacher. His models of human behavior have enriched my personal and professional life. Throughout our twelve years of working together his critical scrutiny of my views have always refined my thinking. I feel fortunate, for he has taught me to see the world as organized, to recognize that everything is interelated and that there is nothing more fundamental.

I want to thank William Polm for his editorial suggestions. I also appreciated the technical suggestions given by Raymond Choiniere. I owe special acknowledgement to Roger McGookin of Fountain Valley Unified School District, Linda Berens of Ocean View School District, Gina Lamphere of Corona-Norco Unified School District, Cynthia Morgan of Covina-Valley School District, and Rick Triplett of Irvine Unified School District for assisting with the research on the Learning Pattern Assessment.

My thanks to Doris Ruud of Upland School District and Aileen Manley of Westminister School District for their stimulating and useful suggestions. A special recognition is due to the many participants in my training workshops in West Orange County Consortium of Special Education, Irvine Unified School District, Fountain Valley Unified School District, Westminister School District, Newport-Mesa Unified School District, and Covina-Valley School District.

And, to Ann Foster, thank you for your useful technical suggestions and especially for your caring and support during the writing of this book.

Preface

As a school psychologist and subsequently as a consultant to and trainer of teachers, counselors and school psychologists, I discovered that although my colleagues were attempting to meet the learning and personal needs of students, there was a need for a more systematic approach to matching the educational program to the abilities and attitudes of students.

This book provides a description of an efficient and practical approach to engineering the teaching and learning process so that each student has the opportunity to reach his finest achievement. The book is primarily a result of my exposure to and utilization of the theoretical and practical aspects of Keirseian Temperament Theory and Kurt Lewin's Social Field Theory. Keirseian Temperament Theory provided a way to conceptualize the student as an organized dynamic personality. A personality which predisposes the student to certain ways of thinking, wanting, liking and acting. One which also gives the student a unique learning pattern. Social Field Theory provided a method for conceptualizing and analyzing the student and his environment as a single unit, as interdependent factors.

Over the years I have discussed most of the ideas and practices presented in this text with educational practitioners. Many were willing to test the ideas and practices in their work with students. This provided an important part of the groundwork for this book. Their encouraging feedback and desire for more information gave me the incentive to continually refine my thinking. Eventually I designed a series of workshops to assist them with the application of Keirseian Temperament Theory in motivating and controlling student learning. Response to the workshops was positive.

This text was written to meet requests from educational practitioners who are interested in gaining an understanding of the personality types and learning patterns of students.

The book gives a step-by-step approach which will enable the practitioner to identify each student's personality style and learning pattern and then to use this understanding in systematically planning each student's educational program. The identification of a student's learning pattern can be as useful to the practitioner as is the mathemaical formula used by the scientist. In knowing a student's personality style and learning pattern the practitioner will be able to understand why the student does what he does, and to predict how he will respond to various conditions of the classroom. It is the student's personality style that determines which instructional methods will be most effective, the kind of circumstances he needs in order to master material most easily and the kind of classroom atmosphere which will stimulate his interest, responsiveness and cooperation. To get a student to take more responsibility for his learning we must first appeal to his natural way of being. We must adapt to his nature rather than try to alter him to our wishes.

I hope that the book will not only give valuable and practical assistance to educational practitioners, but that it also will serve as another stepping stone in bringing together psychological and educational practices.

In this book, "he" refers to persons of either sex. I hope this word choice will be acceptable to all readers. The use of the word "is . . ." in the text that follows means that I have a solid belief about something, based on my own experience as a practitioner or on the experience as a practitioner or on the experience of others. To say "it seems to be . . ." or "it appears to be" means that I am waiting for further evidence before taking a firm stand.

—Keith Golay

I

Overview And Summary

The Problem: Reducing Mismatch

Nowadays educational practitioners are expected to do more with less. Not only are they to teach a diversity of students individually, but they are to teach these students a wide variety of skills and knowledge. And, it is expected that a good teacher will not only welcome the challenge but will know exactly how to carry it out!

- How can I get more students to do their homework?

- How can I get students to be more cooperative in class?

- How can I develop a better sense of group cohesion?

- How can I get students to take a greater responsibility for their own learning?

These are the kinds of questions that teachers ask themselves. When answers are found it is often a result of trial and error over many years.

The problem is that when the practitioner has to deal with differences between students in an environment as complex as the classroom, there are many ways for incompatibility to occur between the needs of students, the instructional program and the utilization of classroom space. Mismatch occurs. Certain modes of instruction are effective with some students but not with others. Some students show an interest in certain subjects but not in others. And, the atmosphere which motivates some students doesn't motivate others.

A mismatch is a deficiency of match. It is incompatibility between a student and a task, or a task and a space. When a mismatch occurs a degree of unproductive behavior follows. Preventing the occurrence of mismatch is essential if the student is to work to his potential. In fact, many learning problems can be eliminated by providing students with an education program compatible with their pattern of learning.

Some practitioners have attempted to deal with this problem by identifying each student's cognitive ability and then match instruction to that ability.[1] Others prefer to consider each student as having a particular affective attitude and attempt to create an atmosphere which matches it.[2] The approach in this work differs from both such approaches in so far as the emphasis is not on the presence or absence of one fact or a number of facts viewed in isolation. The view presented here is upon the constellation of facts in the specific situation. While this approach assumes that the practitioner must consider the student's way of thinking and liking, the focus is on the relationship between the student (as a total personality) and his classroom environment. The focus is not on the relationship between an isolated trait of the student and some isolated aspect of his environment. The student and his environment are viewed as a whole, as a constellation of interdependent factors.[3] Adopting such a view leads to a different way of thinking about teaching. Before discussing this difference, however, let us return to the problem of matching.

In order to reduce the number of mismatches that occur in the classroom, there are four basic requirements:

● The practitioner needs to know the personal characteristics of each of his students

● He needs to know which aspects of the educational environment are going to have the most direct effect on the behavior of students

● He needs to know which factors of the educational environment are most compatible with each learner's characteristics

● He needs a plan for arranging the classroom to accommodate a variety of students, methods and materials

This is a tall order. To fill it, however, is to create a situation which can elicit the finest achievement of each student.

Student Characteristics

The number of characteristics of a human being is infinite. Many of these characteristics are important to consider if the student is to be properly matched. The characteristics of a person can be divided into four major categories: overt behavior, cognitive behavior, motivational attitudes and affective attitudes.[4] More simply these might be called doing, knowing, wanting and liking.

What the practitioner needs to know is what sort of person the student is. What, for example, are his characteristic ways of thinking? Is he a conceptual thinker or a concrete thinker? A person who is effective at conceptual thinking may not be effective at concrete thinking. A person who is a practical thinker may not be an effective conceptual thinker. A person might be good at designing or inventing but not effective in remembering isolated facts.

Psychologists have analyzed the dimensions of cognitive abilities and have revealed a number so large that it is overwhelming. There are a similar number of action abilities, motivational attitudes and affective attitudes. Confronted with so many possibilities, the practitioner is likely to throw up his hands in despair and complain that this is all too complicated to consider. The tendency would then be to revert to mere random match or matching solely on the basis of some isolated characteristic. We might ask whether there might be a compromise somewhere between random matching on the one hand and an endless number of characteristics on the other.

Typology. Typology has a history dating to Gnostic philosophy which had the thinking, feeling, and sensing types. During the Greco-Roman era there were the choleric, phlegmatic, sanguine, and melancholic types described by Hippocrates. Each era has brought with it refinements of these forms of being. The belief is that people display a style of life which predisposes them to certain ways of thinking, wanting and emoting and which gives rise to constancies in behavior, and these patterns are recognizable.[5] Knowing a person's personality type enables one to understand and predict his behavior most of the time. Perhaps instead of becoming aware of all of a student's characteristics, the practitioner can become aware of a student's personality type.

The approach taken in this book will be to view the student as a type of personality. The typology which has been utilized is Keirseian Temperament Theory. This is a holistic systems theory approach to the study of personality. In this view personality is conceived as a unity, as organized. It is assumed that the personality functions as a whole, with all its "imagined parts" working together, in an exact relationship to each other. It is this relationship or pattern that is important.

This theory stands in direct contrast to the traditional analytical and summative points of view, which first dissect personality into various *supposed* parts, puts them under the microscope of analysis, and then sums up the parts, hoping for an accurate representation of the whole. Unfortunately, all too often the result of this process is a static compilation of elements that have lost their relationship to each other. Also, frequently, the result is *inaccurate*. The basic mistake is to be found in the assertion that the "elements" of a personality function independently, apart from one another. Thus, the living, vital dynamics of the person, as he functions in reality, are lost.

It is true that one can be aware of a particular aspect of a personality, and identify it as such, but such identification is severely limited in its usefulness when considered in isolation. On the other hand, when the whole is clearly seen, the part, the particular element can be discerned within the whole and in vital contact with the whole.

Trying to understand a "part" of personality, separate from its relationship to the whole person, is like trying to understand the function of the left side of a triangle without considering its relationship to the other two sides. Both "parts," in either case, belong to the same descriptive unit. They have meaning only in relationship to the whole. Furthermore, to see personality as a systematic whole guards against the exaggeration of any one supposed element, and the other resulting detrimental biases (e.g., where one person judges another person's behavior as "bad" and concludes that the person is "totally bad").

Classroom Environment

As stated previously, the student does not exist in empty space. He is a member of a classroom which has a daily rhythm. At times he is alone or in a group, studying or playing, being encouraged or discouraged, completing a workbook or writing a story, sitting at a desk or standing at a table. Somehow all of these factors affect his learning behavior at any given time. These environmental factors influence each student's behavior every day.

The behavior of a student is the result of a multitude of external, as well as internal, forces. Some forces support each other, some oppose each other. Some are driving forces, others restraining forces. Those external forces of the classroom environment which have the most direct effect on the student can be classified as: Instructional Strategies, Curriculum Content and Classroom Atmosphere. In essence, the practitioner will have three major variables to consider as he maps out an educational program for students.

Instructional Strategies. Instructional strategies are those methods, maneuvers, tactics or modes of instruction that a teacher uses in order to bring about a specific learning outcome. These methods range from using discussions, demonstrations and lectures, to using assignments, games and exercises. What the practitioner needs to know is what tactics are going to be most effective with which type of learner. Which type of learner, for example, is going to be most responsive to dramatization, role playing, and instructional games? And, will this same student be responsive to workbook completion, and recitation and drill? Also, will a student who does well in competitive activities do well in cooperative activities, and vice versa? And, of course, it would be important to know whether some students perform better when working independently or in small groups.

In selecting instructional methods the teacher will not only need to consider the types of students in his class, but he will also need to consider the nature of the curriculum being used, and the options for scheduling tasks. Certain curriculum content, for instance, might not lend itself to certain instructional tactics. The point is that the selection of strategies cannot be considered out of relationship to the other important environmental variables.

Curriculum Content. Knowing the kind of curriculum content that each type of learner prefers is an important ingredient for designing an effective educational program. Perhaps certain students will show a preference for science over history, or language arts over geography. Some may focus on the mechanics of a subject, while others focus on the relevance the subject has to them personally and to their relationship with others.

Once student preferences are known, the students who do not have a preference for certain subjects become the target. Knowing the preferences of students, the teacher can develop a plan for presenting subjects in a manner that will appeal to these students. For instance, take the subject of math. Certain students are likely to find this subject boring and too technical. If the subject is presented as one of memorizing operations, and if it is organized according to well-structured exercises and drills, these students are likely to be unresponsive and probably will do poorly. On the other hand, if these students are the type who need to personalize their learning, to see a personal significance in the subject, the subject could be presented in a manner which matches this need. Such an approach can have the effect of raising the students' interest and may even result in their doing quite well.

Classroom Atmosphere. The classroom atmosphere is that distinct impression that the environment creates in students. It exerts a definite influence on each student's state of mind, his perspective and his behavior.[6] The classroom may have a friendly, warm and personal atmosphere. Or, the climate may be hostile, defiant and stifled. The classroom will also have a social atmosphere which gives meaning to the situation as a whole. The situation may be one of working, playfulness, or discovery. It could be a situation in which students are very cooperative and act as a cohesive group.

It is important for the practitioner to know what kind of atmosphere or climate needs to be created in order to maximize the responsiveness of each student. Some students may do best in an atmosphere of fun and excitement, others may need a friendly, secure atmosphere, and still others may need a harmonious and democratic atmosphere. The key to creating a variety of classroom climates will ultimately be contingent upon the kind of relationship the teacher establishes with students.

Classroom Design

Having knowledge of the characteristics of students, the characteristics of the classroom environment and the compatibility or match between the students and the environment, the practitioner will then be able to identify the spatial requirements for accommodating a variety of students, methods, and materials. After considering how to match students to tasks, the practitioner must determine how to match tasks to spaces.[7] First, he must select the kinds of materials and tasks that are to be utilized and second, he must plan how task spaces are to be arranged. The arrangement of task spaces should be based upon such things as the requirements of the activities, the scheduling of activities, and student needs for privacy.

Teaching To Type vs To Individual

Earlier it was mentioned that, when one views the student and his classroom as a constellation of interdependent factors, there evolves a different way of thinking about teaching.

In the view offered here, teaching is not considered to be a process which occurs independently of the student. Rather it is a particular kind of relationship between the student as a personality and his educational environment. The quality of this relationship is contingent upon the degree of compatibility that exists between the student's way of thinking, wanting, liking and acting, and such environmental factors as instructional strategies, curriculum content and the classroom climate.

When the teacher begins to view each student as having a certain type of personality and a particular learning pattern he will no longer expect all students to be responsive to the same educational program. Nor will he attempt to teach each student individually. Once a student's learning pattern is identified, the teacher can group students according to their similar learning patterns and teach students within each group via the same instructional methods and materials. Thus, rather than having one instructional program for all students, or a separate instructional program for each student, the practitioner who utilizes the approach presented here designs four instructional programs—a program to match each of the four temperament styles.

NOTES AND REFERENCES

1. Robinson, Jack E., and Jerry L. Gray, "Cognitive Styles as a Variable in School Learning." *Journal of Educational Psychology,* 66, 5 (1974): 793–799. Lawrence D. Brown and Floyd McCain, Jr., "The Effect of Cognitive Style in Verbal and Practical Concept Formation Tasks." *Educational Resources Information Center, Washington, D.C.; U.S. Department of Education,* (February, 1971), ED. 030 553. Richard H. Coop, "Effects of Cognitive Style and Teaching Method on Categories of Achievement." *Dissertation* Abstracts, XXIX, Indiana: Indiana University, 1968:2110–A.

2. Dunn, Rita, and Kenneth Dunn. *Teaching Students Through Their Learning Styles: A Practical Approach.* Reston Publishing Company, A Division of Prentice-Hall Publishing, Inc., 1978. John F. Howell and Marilyn Erickson, "Matching Teacher and Learner Styles." Toronto, Ontario, Annual Educational Research Association, 1978. *ERIC* Document Reproduction No. ED 151341.

3. The significance of focusing on the interdependency between the person and his environ-

ment is described in the writings of Kurt Lewin. He has emphasized that behavior depends neither on the past nor the future but on the present field, which includes the individual as a personality and those aspects of his environment which have direct effect on his behavior. Lewin expressed this interdependency in his formula of $B = f(P,E)$. This means that behavior is a function of the relationship between the personality of the individual and his environment. This formula has become the keynote of the field-theoretical approach. See, Kurt Lewin, *Field Theory in Social Science*. Chicago: The University of Chicago Press, 1976.

4. Researchers have identified more than 128 types of abilities and attitudes. See, David Keirsey, "A Polarity Theory of Intelligence." Unpublished Ph.D. dissertation, Claremont Graduate School, 1968.

5. Keirsey, David, and Marlyn Bates. *Please Understand Me: An Essay on Temperament Styles*. Del Mar, California, Prometheus Publishers, 1978.

6. The Adlerian Psychologists have been emphasizing the importance of the classroom climate for years. For a detailed discussion of their point of view see, Rudolf Dreikurs, Bernice Grunwald, and Floy Pepper, *Maintaining Sanity in the Classroom*. New York: Harper & Row, Publishers, 1971.

7. The study of how space influences behavior is called, "Proxemics." This is a term coined by Edward T. Hall and is described in his book, *The Hidden Dimensions,* New York: Anchor Books, 1969. I first applied the concept of proxemics to the classroom situation in an unpublished paper entitled, "Classroom Proxemics," 1972. In this paper I discussed the importance of matching the student to tasks and tasks to space.

II

Keirseian Temperament Theory

Since the beginning of time we humans have been interested in ourselves; and as long as psychology deals with us, and not with abstractions, it is absorbing as a drama of which we are the principal characters. Who are we? Why do we do what we do? What drives and compels us to do thoughtful, as well as tragic things? What is personality? Can it be changed? Let us forget everything else for a moment, and inquire into the nature of personality, analyzing and understanding its form.

Throughout history people have observed human differences and have attempted to classify these differences. Gnostic philosophy established three types corresponding perhaps with three basic psychological functions: thinking, feeling and sensations. In 1795, Schiller conceptualized two psychological types, the "Idealist," and the "Realist"; Nietzsche (1871) proposed the "Appollonian" and "Dionysian" types; Spitteler (1881) described two types called "Prometheus" and "Epimetheus." In 1911, William James characterized two temperaments called the "Realist" and the "Empiricist," or what might be better called the "Intellectual" and the "Sensational." Then in 1923 Jung's crowning work on functional types was presented to the English-speaking world in his book, *Psychological Types*. Shortly after Jung's book, Ernest Kretschmer (1925) published his book entitled, *Physique and Character,* and specified the Cycloid and Schizoid types. In 1942, William Sheldon published his work on temperament styles. Then a major breakthrough in the study of typology came in 1962 with the emergence of the *Myers Briggs Type Indicator*, which is an elegant model designed and developed by Isabelle Myers.

Our present concern, however, is not with historical landmarks, except in so far as they suggest that those who have studied people have observed certain differences, and that these differences have been classified in such a way that it provides hope for some scientific order in the study of personality. Our present concern is how we will observe, classify and understand human differences. And, more specifically, how can the educational practitioner utilize his understanding so as to maximize the learning of each student.

The theory of personality we are interested in here, namely the Keirseian Temperament Styles, is a systems approach to the study of personality. According to this model, understanding of an individual as a personality is not to be sought in some specific feature but in the *form, style, configuration* or *pattern* of the whole person, seen in action in real life situations. Keirsey has described different personalities in terms of total behavior-patterns, which he calls *Temperament Styles*.

The Whole Governs The Parts

In this view, "temperament" is the whole individual from the standpoint of behavior, and transcends the activities of its parts. "Temperament," says Keirsey, "can denote a moderation or unification of otherwise disparate forces . . . a kind of thematization of the whole, a uniformity of the diverse."[1] It is "the inborn form of the living being."[2] Temperament is primary; abilities, preferences, emotions and actions are secondary. One's temperament predisposes him to certain ways of thinking, understanding, or conceptualizing, and to having certain wants, motives or values. And, since patterns of emoting and acting are governed by thoughts and motives, they follow suit.

Analogous to the idea of temperament governing behavior is the idea that a square as a whole determines how the individual lines are arranged, or that the artist's conception for a painting as a pictorial unit governs which colors are to be used, or that the composer's conception of a melody as a musical unity determines the notes. In each case, it is the organization that governs the parts.

Very simply, temperament governs behavior. And, by knowing a person's temperament we can predict what he will do most of the time.

Behavior Is Purposive

In this view, it is assumed that all behavior is purposive. The idea of man being a motive-bound creature is certainly not new. Freud believed we were all driven by pleasure, thus satisfying our sexual instinct. Sullivan put social solidarity as the basic craving. Adler saw us as seeking power, thus overcoming our feelings of inferiority. Then there was Maslow, who has us seeking self-actualization. However, each of these authors appealed to a common instinct, motive, or purpose. Keirsey demonstrates that not everyone has the same wish for pleasure or social solidarity or power or self-actualization. Instead, he takes a cue from each of these authors and concludes that certain persons are predisposed to one motive and others to another. He also abandons the concept of instinct for the concept of *self-esteem*. There are those says Keirsey, who like themselves better when they live spontaneously, some hold themselves in higher regard when they achieve social belonging, others look upon themselves with pride as their powers increase and still others like themselves better to the degree they actualize the self. The purpose of behavior, he says, is the achievement of self-esteem, and that which brings this achievement depends on temperament.

In the view presented here, the person is considered to be a unified system of energy. In such a system personality evolves as a whole. Just as a circle was never something else before it was a circle, or as a melody is a unit from its conception, at first the personality is simple, relatively undifferentiated, but a total form. As time passes its complexity increases and its form becomes more obvious. The personality gives direction to the growth and development of the person throughout life. The form of an individual's personality is indelible. It cannot be changed any more than a leopard can change his spots.

The Four Basic Temperament Styles

Keirsey identifies four basic temperament styles: The Dionysian Temperament, The Epimethean Temperament, The Promethean Temperament, and The Apollonian Temperament. And, within each of these styles there are four specific types of personality resulting in a total of sixteen different personality styles. Each type displays characteristic patterns of thinking and desiring underlying and giving rise to constancies in behavior, and these patterns are identifiable. A brief description of the four basic styles follows. For those wishing a more in-depth look at each type, refer to the book, *Please Understand Me: An Essay on Temperament Styles*, by David Keirsey and Marlyn Bates, 1978.

The Dionysian Temperament. Above all else, this person must be *free*. He will not be confined, bound or obligated. To be free of restraints and restrictions, exempt from controls, to be independent, unfettered, to do as he wants when he wants, that is his ideal. For him, "To be pressed into service is to be pressed out of shape" (Robert Frost).

No type is more action-oriented than this one. Not to be able to act, or to have to delay to act creates stress. He is at his worst when forced into a position that restricts his actions. Freedom to act is necessary for his well-being. Action is his thing.

To understand this person we must understand the nature of his action. It is not action which is directed toward a goal. Nor does his action follow a plan. It emerges from his impulses. He thrives and lives on the impulse; it means to feel alive. Where other types tend to ignore or harness their impulses, the Dionysian enjoys discharging them.

Jacques Cousteau, the oceanographer, once said, "It's the doing that interests me. Once it's finished, I'm no longer interested. It's ejaculated, gone forever."

People of this type live in the "here and now." It is an existential approach to life. Each moment of time exists in its own discrete particularity; each moment is new and unique. Charles Lindbergh once indicated that he wanted to spend his life flying because in the air he could "live only for the moment." Life is to be lived day to day, moment to moment, and each day (each event, each moment in each day) is a new experience. And, each day is lived like there is no tomorrow.

Having an absolute involvement in the present is one of the most distinct characteristics of this type. Jacques Cousteau called it "the philosophy of the wind." Rather than having goals, or planning and organizing like others, this person focuses on the "now." If he does have goals, they will be few and tentatively held. If he were to have plans, they would be pragmatic and made on the spur of the moment.

To have goals requires one to wait and to prepare. Planning involves shifting one's attention among the possible alternatives and then directing that attention. When you live in a present-oriented world of immediate specific actualities, the need for goals and plans is minimal.

The spontaneous action of this type may appear to be erratic and reckless by the standards of others. It is nevertheless typically executed with perfect adequacy and, in many cases, even superb competency. In fact, the ability to act swiftly and with precision is what enables this person to be successful in such fields as the arts, business, athletics, law and the military.

The old and familiar hold little interest for the Dionysian. Variety is what he values; it is the "spice of life." He wants to be mobile, to be free to respond to his wanderlust. New experiences are welcomed, such as, trying out new foods, new places to eat and new vacation spots.

"O for a life of sensations rather than of thoughts," wrote John Keats, the poet. The world of the Dionysian is a physical one and it is filled with actualities. The physical and sensual world delight him. He believes that life's resources are to be consumed and used, and his appreciation of sensual pleasures is unrivaled by other types. He usually enjoys good food, good wine, fashionable clothes and beautiful surroundings. The tool is his master and he is compelled to use it. He must fire the gun, fly the plane, race the car, play the instrument, wield the scalpel, brush or chisel. The tool becomes an extension of the self, and it seems to intensify his experience of the moment.

Dionysians frequently are described by friends as "fun-loving, exciting, unpredictable, generous and congenial." Many are charming and witty conversationalists. They enjoy the practical joke and have an inexhaustible repertoire of stories to tell. They have a fraternal outlook and are willing to share their time and possessions with friends. It is a "share and share alike" attitude. Being a good team member is valued if there is a contest, fun and excitement. Loyalty to family, friends and teammates exists as long as there are opportunities for spontaneity and freedom.

In living for the moment and desiring that the experience be intense, the Dionysian will seize the opportunity to take a risk, meet a challenge or to be competitive. Carl Sandberg captured this attitude when he said, "The marvelous rebellion of man at all signs reading, 'Keep Off'." The Dionysian cannot resist such a challenge. This attitude is further illustrated in a comment by a male actor who was asked what he liked about acting:

> It is stardom rather than acting. Stardom is such a game. . . It's so challenging to make the right moves to get your stardom. That excites me. I love the moves, the way it all works, because I can play it, and if I wasn't good at it I would not like it. I like to play, it's very exciting, and I like competition. I like the anxiety, the craziness, the fluster that comes with competition. I like the feeling of dizziness.

Most people who have a reputation for being fearless, someone who faces danger with unflinching courage, are of this type. Crisis brings out the best in this person. And, he evaluates himself on the basis of how quickly, courageously and precisely he can respond. He thrives on crisis, not only because it is an exhilarating experience that calls for taking chances and acting quickly and timely, but because a crisis is usually over quickly, leaving him free to move on to the next experience.

The abilities of the Dionysian person can lead him to great successes or radical breakthroughs in music, art, athletics and science. They also, however, can bring about disastrous follies as in the case of General Custer's last charge. The same quality that allows this type to respond to the moment fully and completely can be disastrous at those times when there is a need to compare the relative significance of events.

The unique abilities and attitudes of this type have produced eminent painters like Picasso and Gauguin, musicians like Beethoven and Rachmaninoff, poets like Robert Frost and John Keats, novelists like Faulkner and Hemingway, politicians like Julius Caesar and John F. Kennedy, generals like Patton and Rommel, athletes like Babe Ruth and Muhammad Ali, industrialists like Henry Ford and Howard Hughes, entertainers like Elvis Presley and Elizabeth Taylor and lawyers like F. Lee Bailey.

The Epimethean Temperament. This type has a longing for *duty*. He exists to be useful to those social units he belongs to. He must *belong*, and he believes this belonging must be earned.

The Epimethean lives in a social world. More than any other type, he recognizes the social nature of man. His interest lies in establishing, nurturing and maintaining social organizations: the family, the church, the school, the hospital, the municipality and the corporation. In fact, he feels bound and obligated to care for and serve these institutions.

The pioneers of the old west are the epitome of the Epimethean Temperament. They were people who sought to tame the west, to establish new social units. They cleared the land, worked the soil, planted and harvested crops, built houses, raised families, and organized and developed communities. They were industrious, dedicated, steadfast and conservative. They were the "salt of the earth," a "pillar of strength."

Structure, order, and planning are values which color most of this type's actions and attitudes. For him, the essence of society is found in its hierarchical structure. There should be subordinance and super-ordinance. There should be rules and regulations which govern the conduct of members. And, one's status in these institutions should be earned.

His desire for social status is strong. The sometimes subtle differences in rank that are awarded people in social hierarchies on the basis of their land, their money, their power and their family do not go unnoticed. While he is willing to acknowledge the status of others and to defer to his superiors, he will equally insist that his own status be recognized and appreciated by superiors and subordinates.

This person tends to relate to others in terms of their status and their public role: as boss, secretary, teacher, student, minister, doctor, patient, etc. When he asks, "Who are you?" he means: what do you do, what is your background, what is your status?

The life of the Epimethean is orderly and routine. He values consistency and, once a plan or schedule is established, he sticks to it and expects others to do likewise. Being places and doing things on time is important, and he tends to become annoyed with those who deviate from time lines. Even present pleasures are not to interfere with one's work toward future goals. In fact, "pleasure is due only when all duty's done" (R. Pollock).

"Everything in moderation" is his motto. A look at how he manages money will serve as a good illustration. Rarely is he extravagant about or indifferent to financial matters. He will watch his expenses, plan budgets, put away savings, avoid debt, compare prices, look for bargains, and will invest wisely. For the most part, he is not erratic or improvident, and manages his life like his budget—thoughtfully and carefully.

Planning for the unexpected is a major concern of the Epimethean. His pessimistic attitude and low tolerance for uncertainty gives him the attitude that he must be prepared, "for who knows what tomorrow will bring." Murphy's Law, which states "whatever can go wrong will," was certainly made with the Epimethean in mind.

As might be expected, this person is not a risk-taker like his reciprocal, the Dionysian. A comparison between Dionysian and

Epimethean military generals illustrates this difference. A general like Patton or Rommel would take great risks to do whatever was necessary to win a battle. Generals like Wellington and Montgomery fought by the rule book and were appalled at the chances their opponents were willing to take. The Epimethean wants to minimize risk. He does not like to be rushed into things and will go to great lengths to plan and organize in an attempt to deal with uncertainty.

The Epimethean's desire for deliberation and planning can be a tremendous asset, but accompanying these qualities is also a reluctance to accept the unfamiliar, the different or the innovative. He relies on the "tried and true." The old and familiar are preferred over the new and revolutionary, even when a change might be more productive.

Living in a world where all things are mutable, the Epimethean's desire for stability and certainty leads him to place a strong investment in preserving the past, as well as conserving the present. He will collect objects representative of past events: photos, notes, diaries, trophies, and the like. Names and faces of people past are remembered. Things like yearbooks, reunions, and tracing the family line are considered important. Just as he loves familiar places and faces, he will be fond of celebrations of the traditional form: Christmas, Thanksgiving, Easter, weddings, christenings and graduations.

Friends of Epimetheans often describe them as "stable, responsible, dependable, and practical." This type has a paternal attitude and feels obligated to take care of and nurture others. He also has a desire to make others into duty-oriented parents and will expend his efforts to get them to be responsible and obligated, just as he is.

This type is truly the stabilizer of the social and economic world. He creates and fosters social organizations. His fundamentals serve as foundations for what and how we erect and preserve our institutions. He is committed to the transmission of the values and mores of society to the next generation. He is most often our teacher, preacher, historian, banker, clerk, accountant, doctor, nurse, lawyer, policeman, manager, salesman—he is driven to conserve.

The Promethean Temperament. The goal of the Promethean is to be *competent;* he has an insatiable desire to acquire intelligence, to store up wisdom. To become capable is his ideal. He must be competent. He is compelled to seek out answers to life's riddles; to increase his knowledge and to develop his skills.

Francis Bacon said, "Knowledge is Power," and so it is for the Promethean. He has a hunger for power—not power to impose his will on others, but power over nature. To be able to understand, explain, predict, and control realities. It is through ideas that he hopes to gain this power. His commitment to theory overrides all other considerations. He believes in acting according to theoretical principles. "Principle is the only safe precedent," said Frank Lloyd Wright.

This type places a high value on intellectual achievement, and he tends to spend most of his life dealing with intellectual matters. Many are scholarly. Nearly all enjoy learning and being a student. A great many become college professors. Paradise for these people would be to have the opportunity to spend most of their time in an inexhaustible library studying, reading and thinking. It would be far easier for the Promethean to go without much external stimulus than to live without a "chance to think." In fact, his compulsion to think can be so great that he cannot turn off the mental activity currently absorbing him.

Certainly, the Promethean is not the only type who enjoys thinking and learning. However, his passion for knowing penetrates all of his relationships to life, thus distinguishing him from the other types. He is not so much interested in acquiring isolated facts, or in understanding himself. Rather he is interested in developing and using theories to explain facts, and in speculating about why things and people are the way they are. Universal ideas interest him as does using theoretical principles and testing his ideas in the real world.

The Promethean is also disposed to being self-critical, perhaps more so than any other type. Precision, consistency and coherence are demanded. He has an unending list of *should knows* and *should-be-able-to's*. Errors in logic are not to be made. He will accept that "to err is human," but to make the same error more than once is totally unacceptable.

When it comes to ideas and analyzing a situation, he displays a great deal of patience. Einstein, who was a Promethean, said "the only attitude is patience." Every possibility must be carefully considered before an idea, theory, or principle can be legitimately dismissed as unnecessary or invalid.

Prometheans like to collect, organize and classify objects as well as ideational principles. Among both children and adults of this type are enthusiastic collectors of stamps and coins. Many may be amateur bird watchers, botanists or geologists—each specimen is carefully collated and correctly identified. As a youngster, they may collect leaves, butterflies or rocks and may have an interest in such things as rocketry and shortwave radios.

Collecting principles brings this type the most enjoyment. Every event is governed by a strong sense of the appropriate theoretical principle involved. As the Promethean encounters a new situation he will look for the principle to be derived from it. Once identified, the same principle will be applied to other such situations.

If he discovers two principles which come into conflict, he will usually handle the problem by deferring his decision in the hope that an overriding principle or a "meta principle" is discovered so a resolution of the apparent contradiction can occur. And, once a principle is embraced, it becomes something sacred. You can ask many things of a Promethean, but never ask him to give up or break one of his principles.

Surely, someone may object at this point and say that everyone has principles by which to live. As used in reference to the Promethean, "principles" are abstract, intellectually derived absolutes, and experientially tend to be particular to the Promethean. For an Apollonian, being authentic will usually take precedence over the principles of the Promethean. The Epimethean will prefer social solidarity, and the Dionysian prefers action. Principles, for the Promethean, comprise his selfhood.

This type has an appreciation for verbal elegance and usually has excellent verbal fluency. In his conversations he will pay as close attention to grammar as he will to syntax. Context and meaning, however, are usually less important—much like the scientist who devises an elegant design which is used to research something inconsequential. He often enjoys using polysyllabic words even when one syllable would do. The dictionary is one of his favorite books. He has a belief in the power of words, and they should always be chosen precisely and pronounced correctly. Even though he usually knows grammar and syntax, he is often not a good communicator. In an attempt to be precise and to say the most with the least, he will use complex words which others frequently do not know and therefore they do not comprehend what he is saying. His communications can mystify others—thus not providing the clarity to others that he claims to value for himself.

Problem-solving is highly valued by this type. Some delight in creating theories to explain problems, others in putting theories into practice to solve them. If we look at such people as Bacon, Newton and Locke we see that their contributions were in the realm of ideas, not deeds. Like these three men, Prometheans are highly capable of logical thought, and developing complex theories. They take pleasure in any work which entails synthesizing the logical elements. For Prometheans—Einstein and Newton, to take lordly examples—it is the theory and its utility for explaining, predicting and controlling realities that is most appealing.

In having the propensity for developing theories, exploring ideas, and building systems, it is not surprising that Prometheans are drawn to occupations which have to do with the formation and application of scientific principles. Science, technology, philosophy, mathematics and logic, design and engineering, research and development—are most appealing to this type.

The Apollonian Temperament. "Each man must discover his own way," said Sartre. For the Apollonian, life is a process of self-discovery. It is a grim thing indeed to live with one's self as if living with the unknown. It is to be selfless, to ignore, evade, repress the personal needs of one's soul. It is to know the least about the things that matter most. And what matters most to the Apollonian? It is that of *becoming* a unique identity.

The Apollonian hungers to be and to become real. To become self-actualized is his goal. To be himself and to have a unique identity. His lifelong search frequently causes him guilt, however, believing that his real self falls short of his ideal self. And so he wanders, seeking to satisfy his hunger for unity and uniqueness. Whether it be in his relationships, his learning, recreating or working, the sense of self-discovery, enhancing and developing his identity is pervasive:

> In acting you use your whole person . . . I like to develop my personality. It is satisfying and very rewarding to do something well . . . It also is marvelous for the ego . . . If I were not in this industry there are facets of me that would remain untapped, buds that would never ever blossom, and I suppose that there are buds that won't blossom because I am not doing something else, but I like this flower. (Actress)‑

To be one of the "herd" is to be nothing. To not be recognized as an individual who makes unique contributions is to not be at all. In all aspects of the Apollonian's life, he must have *meaning*. He wants others to appreciate his significance. He would rather be loved for who he is than what he has accomplished. Marilyn Monroe, for example, has been quoted as saying, "I wanted to become famous so that everyone would like me and I'd be surrounded by love and affection." This type of person's well-being is contingent upon receiving from others an appreciation (or love if you will) for being "himself"—for being sensitive, open and responsive to the "good" things in life.

Apollonians have a profound sense of personal integrity, which is to feel consistent, unified. There must be no facade, no pretense. They seek to be genuine, to communicate authentically, to be in harmony with the inner experience of self. To be inauthentic, unfaithful to one's real self, is to lose the self and to live a life of bad faith.

Consciously or subconsciously, explicitly or implicitly, the Apollonian seeks a comprehensive view of existence to integrate his values, to choose his goals, to plan his future, to maintain the unity and coherence of his life—and metaphysical value-judgments are involved in every moment of his life, in his every choice, decision and action.

An Apollonian's sense of life is formed by a process of emotional generalization, which is a method of classifying and unifying things according to the emotions they invoke. Such emotional abstractions grow into a metaphysical view of man. The criterion of selection that forms these emotional abstractions is: "That which is important to me." The key concept in his formation of a sense of life is the term "important." It is a concept that belongs to the realm of values, since it implies an answer to the question: Important—to whom? Yet its meaning is different from that of moral values. "Important" does not necessarily mean "good." It means "A quality, character or standing such as to entitle to attention or consideration."[3]

Living a life of significance, doing that which is important, making a difference in the world, does satisfy the Apollonian's hunger for unique identity. For him life is a drama, and each experience is endowed with a special interpretive significance. He is constantly looking beyond the mere events of his life, attempting to grasp the importance of each experience—all in an effort to give deeper meaning to his life.

The Apollonian is first and foremost *people-oriented*. His focus is not on social institutions, as it is for the Epimetheans, but is on individuals and their relationships to one another. He seeks personal transactions with others and is committed to assisting them in their own personal growth. It is his nature to look for and to find the potential in others and to nurture and to bring out these possibilities. In this he is like a catalyst and brings out otherwise latent potentials.

Personal relationships are highly valued, for it is through these relationships that they attempt to make a difference in the world and to express their unique identity. The Apollonian's attitude about relationships is illustrated in a passage by Carl Rogers, one of the more able exponents of the Apollonian way. Although in the following passage Rogers is speaking in reference to the therapeutic relationship, the attitudes he expresses are held in high regard by Apollonians:

> First of all one question is, "Can I be real in the relationship." This has come to have an increasing amount of importance to me over the years. I feel that genuineness is another way of describing the quality I would like to have. I like the term "congruence," by which I mean that what I'm experiencing inside is present in my awareness and comes out through my communication. In a sense, when I have this quality, I'm all in one place in the

relationship. There's another word that describes it for me. I feel that in the relationship I would like to have a transparency; I would be quite willing for my client to see all the way through me, that there would be nothing hidden. And when I am real in this fashion that I am trying to describe, then I know that my own feelings will often bubble up into awareness and by expressed; but be expressed in ways that won't impose themselves on my client. The second question I would have is, "Will I find myself praising this person, caring for this person?" . . . a praising of this person as a separate individual. You can call that quality acceptance, you can call it caring, you can call it a nonpossessive love if you wish . . . Then the third quality. "Will I be able to understand the inner world of this individual from the inside?" "Will I be able to see it through her eyes? Will I be sufficiently sensitive to move around inside the world of her feelings, so that I know what it feels like to be her?"[4]

The Apollonians have a desire for and capability to inspire and transform people. Their ability to speak and write fluently is greater than the other types, and its often done with a poetic flair. Many novelists, dramatists, screen writers, playwrights, journalists, and poets are of this type. Their writings deal with such questions as the meaning of life, what is significant for mankind, and display a desire to preserve and develop the good in mankind. For instance, the writings of such great novelists as Ayn Rand, Victor Hugo and Dostoevsky, and such playwrights as Frederick Schiller and Edmond Rostand show a concern for man's soul. They are concerned with moral values and with the power of moral values in shaping human character. The actions that take place in their stories are related to moral values. The events of their plots are shaped, and characters are motivated by their values, by their struggle in pursuit of spiritual goals and by profound value-conflicts.

The interpretive arts, the arts which involve verbal and written communication, become a means for the Apollonian to selectively re-create reality according to his metaphysical value-judgments. They enable him to concretize his fundamental view of man and of existence, and are a means of communicating to man which aspects of his experience are to be regarded as essential, significant, important.

Ayn Rand, for instance, expressed that the motive and purpose of her writings was the projection of an ideal man. The portrait of a moral ideal was an end in itself. A passage in *The Fountainhead* summarizes this goal. Howard Roark explains to Steven Mallory why he chose him to do a statue for the Stoddard Temple:

> I think you're the best sculptor we've got. I think it, because your figures are not what men are, but what men could be—and should be. Because you've gone beyond the probable and made us see what is possible, but possibly only through you. Because your figures are more void of contempt for humanity than any work I've seen. Because you have magnificent respect for the human being. Because your figures are the heroic in man.[5]

The Apollonian has the desire to develop man's greatness, intelligence, virtue and heroism, and to rid him of misery, disease and evil. This desire leads him into such professions as psychiatry, clinical and counseling psychology, the ministry and teaching. These professions provide him with the opportunity to assist others in becoming kinder, warmer, and more loving human beings. In these professions he exhibits a sense of mission, using his creative efforts to win followers for his cause.

Summary

1. Before personality can be understood, it must be observed as a whole. Personality has form. It is the total configuration or pattern of the whole person, and is called Temperament.
2. The parts of personality, called traits, have a relationship to one another, and have meaning only in relationship to the total personality. A trait in one person means quite a different thing from the same trait in another person of a different personality.
3. Temperament is primary, and predisposes the person to certain ways of thinking, wanting, emoting, and acting. Thus, each of the personality styles has its own way of learning, its own way of being motivated, its own way of relating with others, and its own way of being satisfied.

4. Each personality type is constantly striving toward the goal of self-esteem. Each type has a hunger which must be satisfied daily. Some seek to be free and spontaneous, others to achieve social belonging, others to achieve competency, and others seek to gain recognition and personal value. If a situation arises which threatens the individual's self-esteem, he will take defensive action to preserve that which he values and needs.

5. Personality evolves as a whole through the process of differentiation, and as it becomes more complex its form becomes more obvious. To ask a person to change his personality, to not be who he is, is asking the impossible. Attempts to change the personality will result only in diminishing the effectiveness of the personality as a whole.

6. Four different forms of personality can be described, with each type giving rise to four additional types resulting in a total of sixteen different personality types. Each style displays a particular behavior-pattern which is recognizable, identifiable. Knowing an individual's personality type makes it possible to predict what he will do much of the time.

NOTES AND REFERENCES

1. Keirsey, David and Marlyn Bates. *Please Understand Me: An Essay on Temperament Styles*. Del Mar, California: Prometheus Publishers, 1978. p. 27.

2. Ibid., p. 28.

3. Stein, Jess, ed. *The Random House Dictionary of the English Language*. 7th ed. New York: Random House, 1966.

4. This passage is from the film, *Three Approaches to Psychotherapy: Part I: Dr. Carl Rogers*. Santa Ana, California: Psychological Films, 1979.

5. Rand, Ayn. *The Fountainhead*. NY: The Bobbs-Merrill Co. 1943, p. 349.

III

Four Types of Learners

In the previous chapter we briefly inquired into the nature of personality. The basic principles were presented for guiding us in the study of the student as a particular type of learner. Utilizing Keirsey's four personality styles, four basic types of learners can be described, with each displaying distinct learning patterns. Since the major focus here is on learning behavior, the four basic types will be re-named according to their pattern of learning: The Dionysian Temperament is an *Actual-Spontaneous Learner*, The Epimethean Temperament is an *Actual-Routine Learner*, The Promethean Temperament is a *Conceptual-Specific Learner*, and the Apollonian Temperament is a *Conceptual-Global Learner*.

What follows is a portrait of each of the four types of learners. Understanding the basic nature of each learner and being able to clearly differentiate between them will be important if an effective educational program is to be designed and implemented.

A word of caution before proceeding is in order. Any symbols or words of description, in actuality, are generalizations, standing inadequately as a representation of the specifics of the reality they point to. This is also true of the following descriptions. Therefore, do not overestimate these descriptions: It remains necessary for you, the practitioner, to attend to and apply your own experience to the task of understanding learning behavior, and to the next step as well—seeing that understanding gives birth to effective applications in specific cases. Be careful not to lose sight of the student amid the many words of description.

Think of the material in this chapter and in the remaining text as a map, to be used as a guide for your own observations, explorations, and conclusions in a new territory—that of learning patterns. With this perspective, balanced by your own educational experience, this book can be a helpful tool in your study of how to maximize the achievement of each type of learner.

Portrait of the Actual-Spontaneous Learner

Of all types the *Actual-Spontaneous Learner* (ASL) is the least interested in cultural and intellectual matters. William Faulkner and Robert Frost never finished college, and Hemingway chose never to go. It is not that this type is unintelligent; rather they tend to be uninterested in theoretical concepts, the abstract, and formal intellectual structures. In fact many of this type have a negative attitude toward conceptualizing. Hemingway, for example, often mocked intellectuals as weak, cowardly "eggheads".

Nore does this type trust abstractions. Their interest is in dealing with physical realities. We learn, said John Keats, not by "law and Percept," not by "irritable reaching after fact and reason," but by "sensation and watchfulness." The *ASL* prefers to learn from experience, for he considers it to be the best teacher.

The *ASL* is not interested in or motivated by logic or plans. His motivation comes from those actualities that get him what he wants. And what does he want? Most of all, he wants to be free to act spontaneously, without restraints. He does not want to learn, to know, to understand, or to think. His wants are not compatible with the traditional system of education. *Doing* is his thing. As far as gaining knowledge or learning, these become by-products of his actions.

To acquire knowledge for its own sake holds little interest for the *ASL*. For him, knowledge only has significance when it has immediate relevance: only when it enables him to take an action that otherwise could not be taken, or to get something otherwise not obtainable. His attitude is one of, "Why should I learn something if I cannot use it in the here and now?" Since he views the past as dead and the future as unrealized, only the now exist, and it is the now that must be lived.

> David entered the fifth grade labeled as a "non-reader." The teacher soon discovered that if David was to learn to read he would do so only as a result of being engaged in some activity which required reading in order to reach an immediate personal gain. Such an opportunity occurred one day when several students were discussing their science project. One of the students wanted to demonstrate the working of a doorbell. He had the proper materials but the bell didn't work.

> David asked if he could try to fix it. The teacher decided to let him respond to the challenge and told him to go ahead and gave him the directions in the science book, knowing that he could not read. Within minutes David had the doorbell working, despite his inability to read the directions in the book. He was asked to explain to the class how he fixed the bell. He face showed excitement.

> At the end of the day the teacher talked to David about whether he would like to look through the books on electricity and see if there were any experiments he would like to demonstrate to the class. He took the books home to determine the tools and materials he would need for his chosen experiments.

> The next day he indicated that he didn't know a lot of the words. The teacher began to help him. For the first time the printed word took on meaning for David.

The *ASL* lives for the moment. He does not want to conserve, plan, or organize. He wants to live life as freely as possible. As classwork becomes a matter of study and preparation, he becomes disinterested. As the demands for concentration increases and activity decreases, he becomes bored, restless, and begins to turn to activities of his own choosing. Lindbergh, for instance, couldn't understand why anyone should "spend hours of life on formula, semicolons and on crazy English." He could sit and concentrate for so long "and then, willy-nilly, my body stands up and walks away."

In the typical classroom students are required to control their impulses, to follow a structured routine; they often are restricted or confined to a limited geographical area; they are to move about in an orderly fashion. The *ASL* is impatient with such formal structures. He needs to be free to move about. And, since he rejects and rebels against being "fenced-in" he is often unsuccessful in formal schooling. William Faulkner could not tolerate the enclosure and regimentation of the classroom. He wanted to be free, unrestricted, unrestrained and, as could be expected, he dropped out of high school.

Rather than tolerate the regimentation of the educational system, this student is likely to leave school as soon as possible. Situations which attract him involve action, excitement and freedom. It is quite understandable why this group tends to terminate their formal education with high school. They are likely to instead become the racer, the surfer, the skier, the artist, the actor or the entertainer. They gravitate toward such jobs as construction worker, truck driver or machine operator. Many enjoy being the promoter, negotiator or entrepreneur. They are most successful in occupations which demand action and freedom to respond to the moment.

It is not that this type cannot learn. It is that they feel restricted and restrained by the structure and routine of the educational system. "A school boy," said Robert Frost, "may be defined as one who can tell you what he knows in the order which he learned it." His remark may be disingenuous, but the underlying attitude is typical of the *ASL*.

The *ASL* can become a "behavior problem" in a classroom which demands that he sit quietly in his desk for a long time, or that asks him to follow a long list of classroom rules, or to only have teacher-student interaction, or to work for long periods on paper and pencil tasks. This situation so mismatches the *ASL* that he begins to resist, and becomes uncooperative. He can be an attendance problem, disrupt the classroom, refuse to do his work and act defiant.

With the *ASL's* need for variety, he easily becomes bored and requires continuous stimulation. Not only will he dislike things that go on too long, he will dislike repetition and drill. Premack[1] discovered that students are more likely to engage in activities which they perceive as undesirable, i.e., doing arithmetic, reading and the like, if following such activities they are given equal time to do activities of their choosing. This could be a very useful approach for motivating and preserving the cooperation of the *ASL*.

Also, over stimulation can be a problem for this student. It is better to intersperse quiet, solitary and relaxing activities with exciting and more stimulating ones. He will enjoy frequent changes from individual to small-group to large-group activities. If work patterns are varied each day he will be more responsive. Randomness is welcomed. He will be ready to take time out for relaxing, joking around and having fun. This tends to be disruptive to the more orderly students, especially the *ARLs*.

There is a positive side to the *ASL's* propensity for acting on impulse: He can be caught by his action-hunger and develop skills which come only from excited concentration on an activity for long periods of time. Living only for the moment, he can develop perfect action and without ever practicing like other types do. He does not practice to achieve perfect action, and yet he can achieve it. He simply spontaneously acts, endlessly, having no end beyond the doing.

Once an activity captures his interest he can do it for hours on end. He can spend day after day manipulating objects or using a tool. He can spend hours playing a musical instrument of his choosing—only to lose interest as spontaneously as it was captured. Those who do not lose interest become the outstanding artisans and adventurers. Tasks which involve performing, manipulating, constructing, operating and disseminating generally can interest this student, but if school work becomes a matter of preparation, acquiring rules and facts through reading and writing, his interest wanes.

> Tom was an indifferent student. He would sit with his feet on his desk and a
> defiant look on his face. He rarely paid attention in class but occupied

himself by breaking his eraser into small pieces and throwing the pieces at other students. He also threw spit balls.

One day the teacher discovered that Tom made frequent trips with his uncle on a large diesel truck. She asked Tom if he would be interested in showing the class the operation of a large truck. Tom's eyes glinted. He got his uncle to bring the truck to the school grounds and they demonstrated its operation to the class. Tom began to show interest in school.

Given variety, and some excitement, the *ASL* is cheerful in the classroom. He can be a constant source of fun and laughter. Many of this type will enjoy entertaining their classmates. They are often bursting with energy to put on a show of some kind. They also like being entertained. In fact, one way to keep this student's attention is to make activities entertaining; and the more entertaining the task, the more likely his interest will be preserved.

ASLs like competition, a contest, or a challenge. They thrive on situations where the outcome is unknown. Games of all sorts will hold their attention, for games meet their need for excitement and action. They must do something if they are going to learn, and the more game-like the task, the better.

It is estimated that this learning pattern makes up approximately 38% of the students in the regular classroom, which means that in a class of 32, there will be approximately 12 *ASLs*.

Portrait of the Actual-Routine Learner

Actual-Routine Learners (ARLs) seek to know those realities, those concrete actualities that will enable them to fulfill their need to establish and preserve social units. They focus on responsibility, on developing good study habits, on developing proper social attitudes and on completing well-structured assignments which have met with teacher approval. The *ARL* gains knowledge through identifying and memorizing facts and procedures, through repetition and drill, and through sequenced, step-by-step presentation of material.

When studying a subject, this student is most interested in the mechanics, the practical aspects of the subject. Whether it be history, geography, english, arithmetic, or science he looks for the fundamentals. Abstractions, theoretical principles are seen as having little direct value, and are not as meaningful as any particular actuality.

In a classroom where there are consistent, clearly defined procedures he will thrive. He needs an environment which is orderly and well-structured. Classroom rules are desired and dutifully followed; and, he expects other students to adhere to these same rules. In fact, he is likely to "police" the behavior of his classmates. If other students do not sit quietly, follow rules, and adhere to the schedule he is compelled to try and correct these deviant behaviors. For instance, the *ARL* in elementary school may say to the teacher, "Billy is talking," "Susie keeps turning around," "Jimmy is getting out of his seat," "Tom hit me," "Bruce didn't throw away his gum like you told him." At a very young age this student can act like a duty-oriented little parent. While other students are having fun acting-up, the *ARL* will be trying to get them to do what they are "supposed to do."

If the *ARL* is asked to invent his own procedures, or given vague directions, he becomes distressed and begins to falter. More than any other type, the *ARL* needs to be given clear expectations and specific procedures for accomplishing a task. When given step-by-step instruction and a routine schedule he does quite well. But if he is required to improvise, guess, or to create something on the spot he has a great deal of difficulty. His way is to plan, prepare, and practice, and to do otherwise goes against his nature.

If a routine or schedule is changed, this student feels distress and will try to correct such deviations. For instance, if the teacher forgets to call roll, to write the date on the board, to turn back corrected work, or if he does not follow the time schedule, the *ARL* is the first to notice and comment on such inconsistencies; and he expects that once he has commented on such errors they will be corrected.

The *ARL* needs to know that what is so today will be so tomorrow. The transitory, temporary or expedient can be unsettling. He instead wants the same situation. A well-ordered, quiet, highly structured classroom is needed if he is to perform productively.

> Kathy had always been a very cooperative student who followed the teacher's directions, and completed her work on time. One year, however, she began to display several problems that alarmed her teacher. She became withdrawn, expressed an inability to do the required work, and generally exempted herself from classwork. The teacher tried various ways to help Kathy but without any success.
>
> Finally, the teacher requested help from the school psychologist. Knowing about differences in learning patterns, he determined that Kathy was an Actual-Routine Learner. He also discovered that the teacher provided students with a great deal of freedom, gave them many choices, frequently changed schedules, encouraged students to do independent projects and held many group discussions.
>
> This instructional approach was distressing to a learner like Kathy. The psychologist discussed Kathy's learning pattern with the teacher. As a result the teacher decided to provide Kathy with concrete step-by-step instructions, specifying his expectations, and provided praise for the product of Kathy's activities. Within a short time Kathy was doing much better in school.

Doing the "right" things is important to the *ARLs*. They want to please the teacher and receive his approval. They like being responsible, dependable, and industrious. Their work assignments are usually complète and turned in on time. In contrast, the assignments of the *ASLs* will usually be incomplete, if done at all. The *ARL* strives to do written assignments at a careful pace, taking time to plan and organize, and to complete the work in a neat manner. The *ASLs*, on the other hand, seek to do written work as expediently as possible, paying little attention to neatness.

Attending to isolated details is easy for the *ARL*. He is meticulous in his work and displays a tendency to stick to things. His peers may even call him "nit-picky." Placing the heading correctly on a paper, for example, brings him satisfaction. He holds high standards of achievement for himself, and takes report cards seriously.

The *ARL* will display a reverence for the teacher (who is an authority figure) and has the belief that he should be respected and deferred to. Classroom standards are valued and adhered to. He will be obedient and will attempt to conform to the teacher's expectations; the teacher's values will be accepted as good values.

As part of his need to belong and to be useful, the *ARL* will show a strong interest in being helpful to the teacher. He would enjoy doing such maintenance chores as emptying wastebaskets, taking out trash, cleaning the blackboard, putting away books, or sweeping the floor. Being a classroom monitor is an honor this student enjoys. His source of pleasure is the approval he is given by the teacher as he performs a task. If there is a job to be done, a task to be executed, a duty to fulfill, the *ARL* is ready to respond. He likes doing extra work and can't refuse the opportunity to be responsible.

This student's desire to be useful also comes in the form of membership hunger. He wants to belong to such social units as service clubs, scouts and student government. All are valued because they signify peer and adult approval.

It is estimated that students with this learning pattern make up approximately 38% of the students in the regular classroom, which means that in a class of 32 there will be approximately 12 *ARLs*.

Portrait of the Conceptual-Specific Learner

The *Conceptual-Specific Learner* (CSL) wants to be able to understand, explain, predict and control realities, and in this sense he can be characterized as the "little scientist." He is interested in seeking out and understanding principles, and tends to collect rules in order to give structure to his cognitive world. He wants to know how ideas are conceived and how they are put together. He is usually not interested in isolated facts, but wants to use theories and principles to explain the facts.

He desires to learn criticism through experiment, to learn the process of inspecting hidden assumptions in thinking, to compare new ideas with the old so that the limitations of the old may explain the importance of the new, and that the advantages of the new may become evident through the inadequacies of the old.

His is a life of serious research and exploration. He learns by creative thinking; each task mastered is discovery. His play is work, and his work is play. He is basically serious and is happy being serious. For this type, reading his first story furnishes a thrill of achievement as great as comes to the scientist who discovers a new comet; his first letters are as important as the writer's first novel. His first addition is as stupendous as the discovery of relativity.

For many students, the unknown is accepted as a part of life and adds a mysterious dimension. The *CSL* views the unknown as a mystery to be unravelled. He is very curious. He has a need to find answers to the many questions he has about people and things. He likes to pursue his inspirations, researching out his ideas until his understanding is satisfied. The *CSL* needs ample opportunity to experiment, to find answers to his questions and to develop explanations for those things that capture his interest. His ideas will not typically, of course, be so grand as those of an Einstein or Newton, but they will usually be well thought out. To solve a problem is satisfying to this student, and conversely, not to be able to solve a problem is distressing.

CSLs have an insatiable need to acquire intelligence and to store up wisdom. They tend to be academic achievers and have high standards for improvement. In fact, the teacher may need to help these students come to terms with the fact that they cannot know everthing. They have a compulsion to improve and are hyper-alert to their shortcomings. If they become overly discouraged, they may give up certain scholastic efforts. However, if they are given sufficient encouragement and the opportunity to discover that certain areas of study may not be their forte, they are likely to see their failures and inabilities in a more acceptable perspective.

Because this type of learner is usually seen as intellectually precocious and displays a high interest in gaining knowledge, it is all too easy for the teacher to give him work beyond his ability. The student may then feel self-doubt and become inhibited. It is also quite easy to assume that all students of this type are smart because of their interest in intellectual matters. However, students within this group will vary in terms of the quality of their thinking. And, since each of these students needs an abundance of success, it is vital that they be provided with materials which match their ability.

The *CSL* has the capacity to focus on a single point for a long time. Precise delineations are made with ease. Because of his sharp, narrowed focus he does not allow his attention to wander, nor does he passively permit it to be captured. He will take pleasure in school work which entails synthesizing the logical elements of a task, or which requires technical documentation and classification.

Learning concrete information or following a routine task will hold little interest for this type. He will quickly become bored and disinterested with repetition and drill exercises. It would not be unlikely for this student to bring to school materials of his own liking if the teacher fails to provide him with such materials.

> Skip was a sixth-grade student. Even though he had superior ability, he was not doing his class assignments. Instead, he would sit in the back of the room and read books and magazines on science and technology, which he brought from home.

> Skip's father also enjoyed science and technology. He was a "nut" about computers, and would spend hours with Skip using and designing programs for their home computer.

> The teacher tried everything she could think of to get Skip to do his assignments, but failed. She knew that he had the ability to successfully do the work, and recognized that he had a great deal of knowledge beyond the level of his peers. However, she also believed that it was important for him to do the same assignments that his classmates were doing. A power struggle evolved. The teacher was determined to not let Skip get away with not doing his work.

> Eventually, Skip became totally unproductive at school. His parents had a conference with the teacher and school principal. A heated debate occurred over whether Skip should be treated differently than his classmates. Finally

the parents placed Skip in a private school which catered to students like him.

This was an unfortunate incident. But luckily Skip was placed in a learning situation which matched his learning pattern. The teacher was doing what she thought was best and so were the parents. Each, from his own perspective, was acting responsibly. And yet, if the teacher could have understood the needs of Skip, the incident may never have occurred.

Many *CSLs* gain a reputation among their peers as being able to explain and understand things, thus they are frequently sought out for counsel on technical problems. However, the *CSL* frequently has difficulty relating with others. He tends to be intellectually competitive, becomes annoyed when others do not comprehend the intricacies of his ideas, and presents an objectivity and detached attitude which others find discomforting. Thus, others frequently see the *CSL* as cold, unfeeling and arrogant. When he does try to relate with peers he will often be more instructional than personal. He has a difficult time expressing emotions and showing affection. It is not that he does not care about others or that he does not have feelings. Rather, he responds out of the belief that the real world is abstract, a mental world, and emotions tend to get in the way. The *CSL* can have very intense emotions, and at times may even feel overwhelmed by them, but rather than express these emotions he resorts to intellectualizing them.

Because the *CSL* tends to act differently than his peers, and usually does not share their interests, he sometimes is labeled as a "Weird-O." As a young boy, Einstein was mocked by his peers and called "Old Father Bore." It is not unusual for other students to find communicating with the *CSL* strange and boring, this being because his communications tend to be terse, compact and logical, displaying precise grammar and syntax. And, while other types are busy recreating or socializing, the *CSL* is usually enjoying a solitary activity, like inquiring into some problem that has caught his interest.

Many *CSLs* are not good at mixing with peers, and of the four types, are the least socially aware. The *ASL* is charming and entertaining; the *ARL* is nurturing and thoughtful; the *CGL* is warm and accepting. The *CSL*, on the other hand, is mystified.

At times the *CSL* may do or say things which are an attempt to be congenial, but which put others off. Thus, this student often becomes an isolate, and can experience a deep sense of loneliness. He needs assistance in acquiring those interpersonal skills which would enable him to successfully satisfy his need for relationships.

Approximately 12% of the students in the regular classroom are of this type. Thus, among 32 students, there will be approximately four *CSLs*.

Portrait Of The Conceptual-Global Learner

The *Conceptual-Global Learner* (CGL) has more of an interest in conceptualizations than actualizations, in what could be than in what was or is. He looks deeply and intensely for the truly meaningful; for those things in the world which are important; for those things which make a difference. He searches for the significance of things and events, and wants to understand their meaning. He is not so much interested in facts themselves, like the *ARL,* or in the explanations of facts, like the *CSL,* rather he wants to understand what is important about the facts, what their significance is in the world.

Instead of attending to technical details, the world for this student is endowed with a special interpretive significance. Reality for him is subjective, thus his learning is also personalized. He is constantly looking to discover how his learning is related to himself and to his relationships with others.

CGLs are future-oriented and think about possibilities. But, unlike the *CSL,* they focus on the possibilities in people rather than the possibilities of principles. These students are fascinated by people's beliefs and attitudes; what they think, what they want, how they feel and how they respond. They enjoy learning about ideas and values, and they tend to look at them more subjectively than objectively.

The cognitive experience of the *CGL* is not one of sharply observed facts and well-developed judgments. His cognitive mode is global. Instead of using articulated principles and step-by-step solutions, he tends to use quick hunches and impressions. And, when he looks at facts he is looking to confirm his impressions rather than attending to the isolated facts themselves. His hunches or impressions may be quite interesting and vivid, but they are not detailed or technical. (Such impressions are only potential distractors for the *CSL,* and probably discomforting ones at that, disturbing his more single-minded concentration.)

CGLs are generally high achievers and do well academically. They often set high standards for themselves and can be caught in a pursuit for the "perfect product." Their creations tend to be an extension of the self and are strongly tied up with their identity. Thus if their product is rejected in the slightest they are apt to be devastated. To reject the creation is to reject the person.

This type is an excellent communicator and enjoys the process of communication. As a youngster he will usually have a spoken vocabulary far beyond his ability to capture his thoughts on paper. Also, he usually learns to read easily. Of all types this student can speak and write fluently, and his communications frequently display a richness in content and creativity.

CGLs live in a paradox. They need to be known, recognized and acknowledged by others, especially by the teacher. Yet, they demand individuality, to be autonomous. These students have a strong desire to be their "own person," but they are highly impressionable, easily affected by the opinions of others and by real or imagined expectations.

A personalized approach will be most compatible with this student. For the *CGLs* to be one of the crowd, to go unrecognized as a unique individual, is to be nothing at all. To be seen as unique and as a person who makes unique contributions is what they seek.

> Karen, an eighth-grader, began having difficulty in school. She would constantly seek attention by doing things which irritated her teachers. Luckily, Karen's English teacher understood her personal and learning needs. One day while reading poetry to the class the teacher noticed a captivated look on Karen's face. This provided a special opportunity to arrange for Karen to gain the sense of importance and recognition that she

needed. The teacher asked Karen if she wanted to read some poetry to the class. Karen read the poetry with a great deal of expression. Soon she was reading poetry each class time. Her classmates admired her and asked her to participate in their activities. Karen no longer engaged in attention-getting behavior.

Friendships are important to the *CGL*. These personal relationships help to make their lives meaningful, and are a means for expressing their unique identity. The more outgoing *CGLs* seek many friends and have a talent for making them. When around their friends they sparkle. They enjoy interacting with friends and will spend a great deal of time and effort maintaining these relationships. Those *CGLs* who are shy and lack good social skills need a great deal of personal attention and encouragement from their teacher(s). They may need assistance in becoming a participating member of the classroom and in meeting new people. Without this assistance they can withdraw and become lonely.

The seeking of companionship, both from peers and elders, is typical of the *CGL*. By implication, he expects companionship from adults (superiors) at his level, yet he expects to learn from them.

Even at a young age, the *CGL* displays superior insights into the intangible, especially into human nature. This type is an expert judge of character when another's character affects him. He will understand attitudes, family relations, the texture and form of an individual's personality long before he has names for what he is observing. He can detect affection and artificiality; sense undercurrents of suspicion, hostility, deceit and disloyalty.

In displaying a personal warmth and responsiveness which draws others toward him, he is frequently sought out by peers when they are having personal problems or feel troubled. His insight and his empathy make others feel understood and accepted. In being sensitive, however, and able to identify with the hurts and suffering of others, he can feel burdened with their problems and become emotionally drained.

CGLs are also vulnerable to criticism and conflict. They will go out of their way to avoid hurting the feelings of others. They are hypersensitive to the slightest gesture or word of rejection—especially from the teacher whom they tend to idolize. In fact, *CGLs* are troubled if any student is rejected, and tend to empathize with the hurts and embarrassments of others. The student thrives in a caring, warm, personal atmosphere and withers in the presence of hostility, conflict, sarcasm and ridicule.

In a classroom where the teacher uses punishment and ridicule as a means of control, some students of this type may become rebellious and use their persuasive skills to turn students against the teacher. This type of behavior would not be motivated by vindictiveness or a desire for retribution, as it could be in the case of the *ASL*. Rather, it would be done in an attempt to improve the situation, to create a more humanistic atmosphere. This student strives for a democratic atmosphere. He believes people should be treated with dignity. He wants everyone to be equal, and believes they are entitled to the same rights and privileges.

An environment of social openness appeals to the *CGL*. He prefers cooperative interactions over competitive ones. When relationships are harmonious and when people are acting in a caring way toward one another he thrives. He will conform to the teacher's expectations if he believes the teacher likes him. Generally, he will present a pleasant and agreeable manner.

It is estimated that approximately 12% of the students in the regular classroom are of this type. Thus, among 32 students there will be approximately four *CGLs*.

Summary

In summary, the four types of learners can be characterized by words and phrases:

The Actual-Spontaneous Learner (38% of the students)

Physical Involvement	Fun Loving
Stimulating the Senses	Bold
Realistic	Adventuresome
Immediacy	Competitive
Spontaneity	Challenge
Expending Energies	Contest
Function-lust	Risk
Free-spirit	Excitement

The Actual-Routine Learner (38% of the students)

Social Belonging	Preparing
Caretaker	Conserving Energies
Giving Service	Being Decisive
Obligation	Step-by-Step Order
Responsibility	Routine
Stable	Policies
Sensible	Rules
Practical	Standards
Planning	

The Conceptual-Specific Learner (12% of the students)

Developing Intelligence	Ingenuity
Being Capable	Critiquing
Possibilities of Principles	Explanations
Impersonal Analysis	Predictions
Being Concise	Technical Details
Building Systems	Classifying
Exploring Ideas	Categorizing
Objectivity	Depth

The Conceptual-Global Learner (12% of the students)

Understanding Self   Insightful
Self-Actualization   Appreciative
Possibilities in People   Imaginative
Empathetic   Speculative
Global   Inspirational
Developing Relationships   Idealistic
Integrity   Personalizes Learning
Subjectivity   Breadth

NOTES AND REFERENCES

1. Premack, D. "Reinforcement Theory." D. Levine (Ed.), *Nebraska Symposium on Motivation*, Lincoln: University of Nebraska Press, 1965, pp. 123-180.

IV

Learning Pattern Assessment

The *Learning Pattern Assessment* (See Appendix A) was designed to provide teachers, counselors and school psychologists with a quick and convenient way to identify a student's learning pattern. The statements in the *Learning Pattern Assessment (LPA)* and the patterns that these statements purport to measure are derived from Keirseian Temperament Theory of personality (See Chapter II).

The *LPA* measures four learning patterns which correspond to Keirsey's four primary personality styles:

Learning Patterns	**Keirseian Temperaments**
Actual-Spontaneous Learner	Dionysian Temperament
Actual-Routine Learner	Epimethean Temperament
Conceptual-Specific Learner	Promethean Temperament
Conceptual-Global Learner	Apollonian Temperament

The instrument can be used with elementary, junior high or high school students. It can also be used with adults who have had some college (or equivalent) education. The *LPA* consists of 40 items, with each item being a behavior pattern which is theoretically more representative of one personality type and learning pattern than another. There are ten items or statements for each of the four types.

The person completing the *LPA* rates the degree to which each item or statement describes the person being assessed. Total scores are then computed with the highest score indicating the learning pattern that the assessor rates as being most representative of the person being assessed.

Instructions For Administering

1. If used with adults, the *LPA* can be self-administered. All necessary instructions are given on the cover page of the assessment.

2. When the *LPA* is used to determine the learning pattern of either an elementary, junior high, or high school student, it should be completed by a teacher, counselor, or school psychologist who has had ample opportunity to observe the student in the learning environment for a period of time.

3. There is no time limit for completing the instrument. An assessor who is familiar with the instrument and with the student being assessed can complete the instrument in 10 minutes.

4. It is important that each item be rated. Do not guess on items. If you do not have sufficient information to make an accurate rating, either observe the student or review his records for possible descriptions of his behavior by previous observers.

Instructions For Scoring

1. The instrument is self-scoring. Both the taking and scoring of the instrument can be completed within 15 minutes; the scoring process taking approximately five minutes.

2. To avoid errors in scoring, double-check the accuracy of both the transferring of the ratings to the score box, and the addition of the points in each column.

3. The total score for each column can be displayed graphically by

plotting them on the chart appearing on the back side of the scoring sheet. The four total scores can be plotted as crosses on the vertical lines on the graph. The four crosses can be joined by ruling a diagonal line.

Interpretation Of Scores

Each of the 40 items or statements has now been rated and scores computed. The column which has the highest total score identifies the temperament style and learning pattern which the assessor has rated as being most descriptive of the student. It can be assumed that the higher the score total for a particular type, the stronger the pattern appears to be for the student. The maximum score that can be obtained for any given pattern is 50.

The greater the highest total score is than the other total scores, the more critical it becomes to provide the student with an educational program which *consistently* matches his particular learning pattern.

It should be noted that a person is not expected to be completely one type of learner or the other. Rather, one can display various behaviors of each type in some degree. Thus in some cases the total scores may be very similar, while in other cases the scores will be quite different.

In addition, it is not expected that a person's behavior patterns will not ever change. Temperament theory postulates that at the core a person will show a tendency toward being one type more than another. But as time passes certain behavior patterns may strengthen or weaken in one direction or another. The personality of the young student, for example, will be relatively undifferentiated. His behavior may be influenced more by those around him than by his natural preferences. As he develops and as his personality becomes more differentiated, his behavior patterns will become more consistent, and his particular temperament style and learning pattern will be more observable and identifiable.

Having identified a student's temperament style and learning pattern, the task now is to read his type description in Chapter II and the description of his learning pattern in Chapter III. As you read these descriptions, decide how well or how poorly they fit the student. If the descriptions do not seem to fit, read the other portraits and determine which one is most representative of the student.

In the case where no single learning pattern has a total score greater than the other patterns, it is recommended that you read the descriptions of those learning patterns which have the most similar total scores and decide for yourself which parts of each description are applicable to the student.

Reliability

The problem of ascertaining the reliability of an inventory or questionnaire is complex. The major problem is one of determining how much of any given result is due to the reliability of the instrument and how much is due to the reliability of the person making the evaluation. For instance, there is the problem of whether the assessor is willing and able to give an accurate report on or response to the items.

In the case where one person is observing and assessing the behavior of another, the first problem has to do with whether the observer has had ample opportunity to observe the subject in a variety of situations so that he acquires a representative sample of the subject's behavior. Second is the problem of determining the degree to which the process of observation itself influences how the subject behaves. The subject may behave differently when being observed than when he is not being observed. The third problem is one of observer/assessor bias. It is the problem of whether the assessor is correctly perceiving the subject or whether he is attributing things to the subject that do not actually exist.

There are also problems when a person makes a self-evaluation. First is the problem of whether the person is reporting in a socially desirable way or reporting on what actually exists. Second is the problem of whether the person knows enough about himself to make a distortion-free evaluation. This problem is frequently not adequately dealt with by constructors of instruments which are to be self-administered by elementary and junior high students.

Faced with such complexity in order to make a reliable assessment of behavior, one might be inclined to say, "Why bother?" Before giving up however one should pause—is it not better that we have some means of observing and assessing behavior, however primitive and general this may be? The alternative is not between having a totally reliable assessment or no assessment, but between degrees of reliability—how much vs. whether.

In an attempt to get an initial determination of the accuracy and precision of the *LPA,* several studies were implemented. The results of these initial studies suggest that the *LPA* is a reliable instrument. However, the data is not absolute.

In the *first study,* a group of 46 students in grades 4-6 was selected. The teachers were then asked to complete an *LPA* on each of their students. Two weeks later a second *LPA* was completed by the same teachers. The highest score in each of the two assessments was compared for each student. In 70% of the cases student's were rated as having the same learning pattern in the second assessment as in the first.

The *second study* was done on a group of 50 students selected from grades 3-8. Two independent raters were then selected for each student. Each of the raters completed an *LPA* on the student to which he was assigned. In each case the pair of raters knew its assigned student equally well. A comparison was then made between the highest score of each of the two raters. In 71% of the cases each pair of raters assessed the student as having the same learning pattern.

Validity

The validity of an inventory or questionnaire is usually defined as "the extent to which the instrument measures what it purports to measure." Problems with determining the validity of an instrument are just as thorny as they are for determining its reliability.

One approach to determining the validity of a new instrument is to compare it with an instrument which is considered to be valid for assessing the same general area of behavior. This approach was adopted for examining the validity of the *LPA*.

An initial investigation was conducted to compare the *LPA* with the Myers Briggs Type Indicator (MBTI).[1] The MBTI is an instrument which measures the same dimensions of personality that are used by Keirsey in the construction of his personality theory. (Keirsey however, analyzed the relationship between these dimensions from a different frame of reference than did Isabel Briggs Myers.)

Since the MBTI is designed for an adult population, and since there is not a similar instrument for young people, the validity study was confined to an adult population.

A group of 90 graduate-level students at California State University, Fullerton, was administered the MBTI. At a later date these same students completed the *LPA*. A comparison was made between the two instruments, and in 80% of the cases the *LPA* identified students as having the same temperament type as the MBTI.

The results of this initial investigation are by no means conclusive but they do suggest that the *LPA* measures what it purports to measure.

NOTES AND REFERENCES

1. Myers, Isabel Briggs. *The Myers Briggs Type-Indicator Manual* Princeton: Educational Testing Service, (Third printing) 1970.

V

Classroom Design: Matching Tasks To Space

The following chapter deals with the question of how to utilize classroom space to provide for the most efficient and effective teaching and learning. It will be proposed here that if people are to behave productively within the classroom, there must be balance between the design elements and the activities to be performed. A variety of classroom spaces are needed, so that the teacher and students can be involved or not, as the occasion and atmosphere demand. The classroom will need to have "semifixed-feature"[1] spaces. Consideration must be given to matching the task to the space and the task to the student.

More specifically, the classroom will need to be arranged in a manner which provides for the following:

● Places were each type of student can work on a task suited to his pattern of learning

● Places where students can work individually, in small groups or in a large group

● Task spaces which allow for a minimum of distraction and disruption

● Task spaces which are arranged so the teacher can instruct, encourage or give feedback on the performance of an individual, small group, or large group while the remaining students are busy.

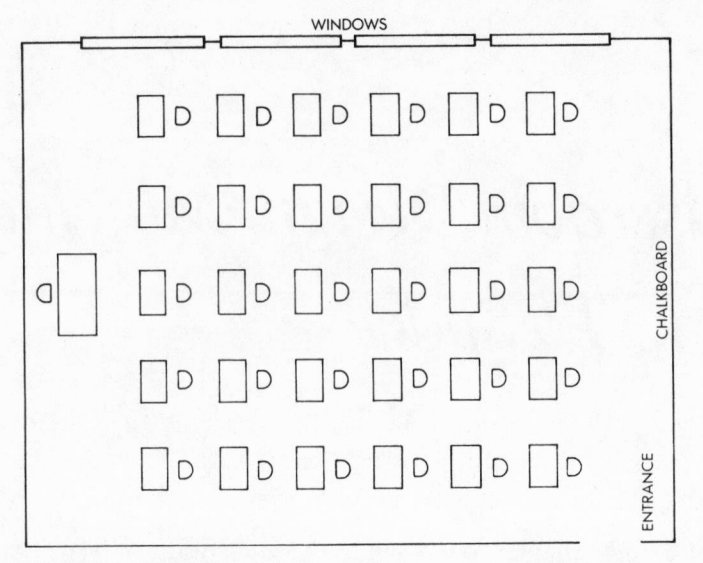

FIGURE 1 When student desks are arranged in rows, students have little privacy and the variety of instructional tasks that can be used is minimal.

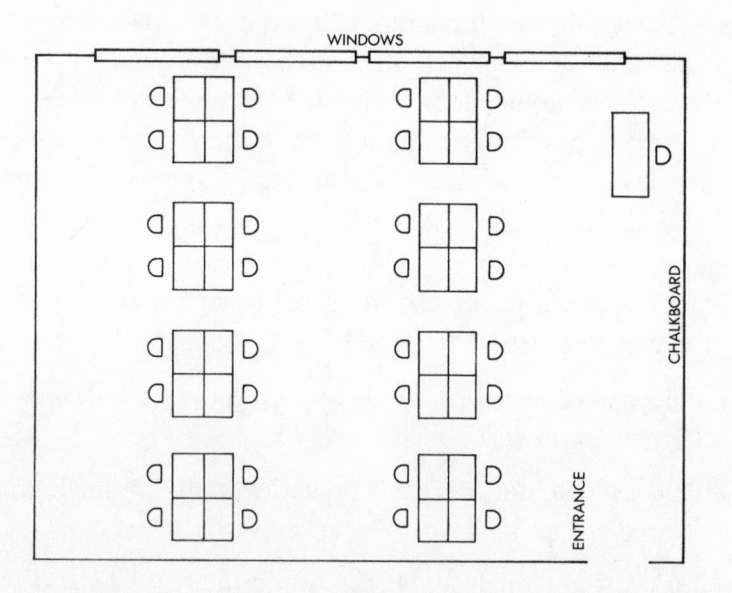

FIGURE 2 When desks are arranged in clusters, those students facing each other can interact much better, but there is also a high potential for distraction. The variety of instructional tasks which can be used is still not sufficient for meeting the needs of all four types of learners.

The question may be asked as to whether existing classrooms can meet the above criteria. The room which has students' desks arranged in rows with the teacher's desk in the front of the room, is a precise organization, but does not allow for mixed functions. There is potential for disturbance and distraction. With this arrangement, students have little privacy, and there can be little variety in instruction (See Figure 1). Then there is the more common arrangement in which tables and chairs are clustered throughout the room (See Figure 2). Here the teacher can feel more certain that students are communicating better because they are facing each other. Again however, the distraction level is quite high. It does allow for slightly more variety in instructional tasks, but not enough to be effective with each type of learner. These two "fixed-feature"[2] arrangements do not seem appropiate, and from a human engineering point of view are illogically deployed for the kind of teaching and learning processes we have been considering in this book.

The alternative is to separate task and match study and interaction tasks to appropriate spaces.[3] Dividing the room in this way is slightly different from the more typical arrangements. However, this spatial rearrangement is no more difficult than rearranging your living room furniture. In both cases the effect can be dramatic, even though the basic contents remain the same.

Creating Task Spaces

What specific kinds of task spaces are going to be needed? This will, of course, be determined by the types of learners in the classroom. If we assume that all four types of learners will be present, we can predict a need for the following kinds of space:

● Places where students can work quietly on such individual assignments as reading a book, writing a report, completing a workbook or programmed materials

● Places where a small group of students can discuss their lessons or work on a group project

● An area where students can meet as a large group for a presentation, discussion or demonstration

● A section of the room where a small group of students can play instructional games

● A place where a small group can work on a construction project or do a science demonstration

● An area where students can view a film, watch an instructional TV program or listen to a record or tape recording.

In order to create these various centers, some type of screening devices will be needed, not only to separate study spaces from interaction spaces, but to separate one study space and interaction space from another.

Screening Devices

Classroom space can be divided by using such available objects as file cabinets, desks, bookcases, shelves, charts, self-supporting blackboards, and screens. These objects can be placed perpendicular to walls, or arranged in the center of the classroom to create various spaces. They also block noise and limit distraction (See Figure 3).

The materials which are to be used in a particular center can be housed in a divider such as a cabinet, shelf, or file drawers. This provides students with easy access to materials and will help keep cross-traffic to a minimum.

Another important screening device is the individual booth or carrel, which can be placed on each individual study desk. It serves the purpose of maximizing concentration and attention, permitting each student to work quietly and independently while at his study station. The carrel is three sided, about 30 inches high, and can be made out of cardboard, quarter-inch plywood, or quarter-inch masonite, and can be designed for maximum flexibility (See Figure 4).

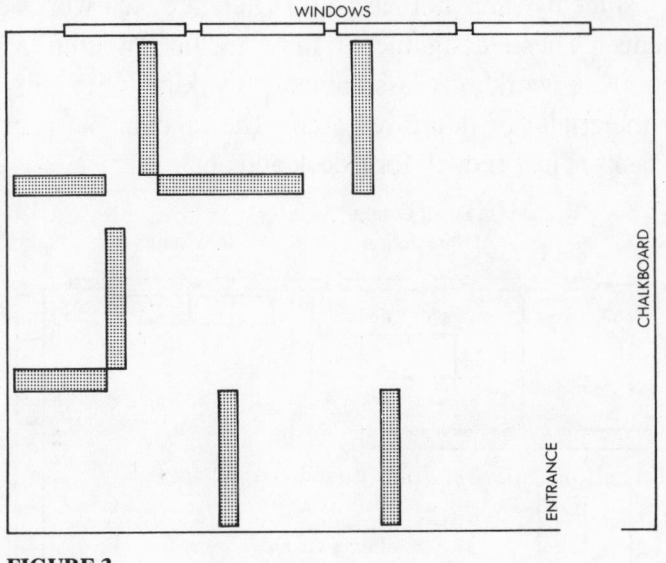

FIGURE 3

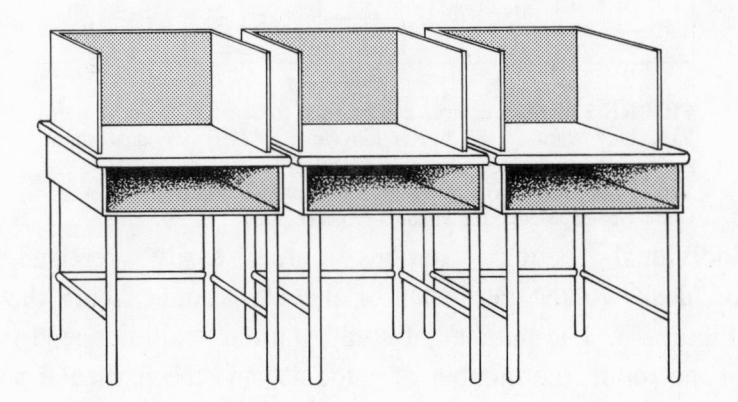

FIGURE 4

Study Spaces

Study tasks require maximum concentration by the student; distraction must be kept to a minimum. While at their study stations, students are not to talk, but are to work on their assignments. These assignments may include writing a play, a book report, a workbook assignment, working with programmed learning materials, or doing research. The amount of space needed for such tasks is just enough for a desk and chair.

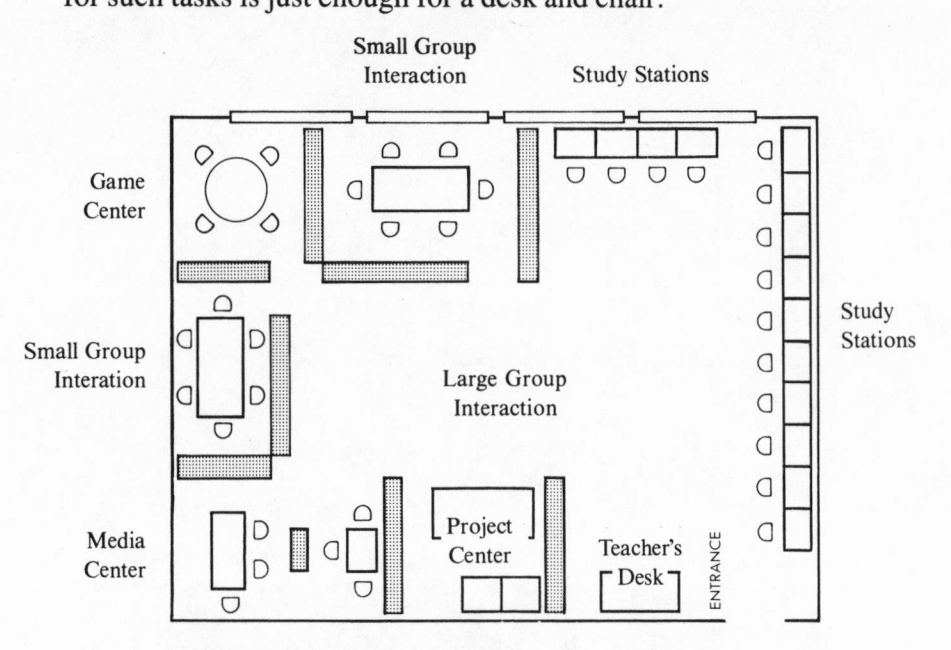

FIGURE 5 Various devices can be used to separate the classroom into study stations and interaction centers. The individual study stations can be located against one wall. Space is now available for large group interaction, several Small Group Interaction Centers, a Game Center, Media Center and a Project Center.

Individual study stations are easily created by moving desks to the perimeter of the classroom, facing the wall (See Figure 5). The number of study stations would depend on the size of the room, the number of students, and the particular subject matter to be covered.

Arranging study stations in this way has several benefits. First, by having the desks facing the wall, the amount of distraction is less. The student can literally turn his back on what is happening in the room and become absorbed in his work. Second, the central space of the room can now be used for large interaction space.

If needed, additional study stations can be created by utilizing portable partitions which can be placed on a table in one of the interaction centers (See Figure 6). When the study stations are not in use, the partitions can be removed and the tables used for interaction tasks. The portable partitions can be made of either cardboard, quarter-inch plywood, or quarter-inch masonite.

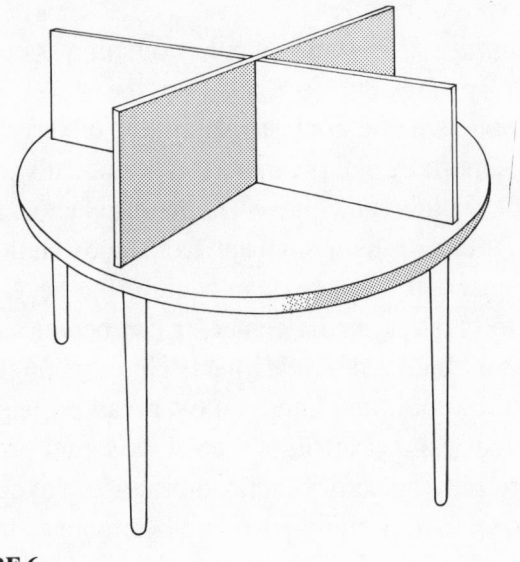

FIGURE 6

Interaction Spaces

Interaction tasks require more space, and the utilization of more furniture, materials and equipment than study tasks. Once study spaces are set up, the central space of the classroom can be divided into interaction centers. For instance, there might be an area for large group interaction, several Small Group Interaction Centers, a Game Center, a Media Center and a Project Center. Each area can be separated from the others by screening devices (See Figure 5).

Large Group Interaction Space. The area best suited for large group interaction is the center of the classroom. It is an area where students can come together for a presentation, discussion, or demonstration. If chairs are needed they can be easily acquired from the surrounding task centers and returned at the end of the large group session.

Small Group Interaction Space. This area can provide students, particularly *CGLs,* the opportunity to discuss their lessons, to have personal interaction, or to do problem-solving tasks. The center may consist of a table and four to six chairs. On one side there may be a shelf or cabinet which houses curriculum materials for various ability levels and different types of learners.

Game Center. This center would contain various instructional games, primarily ones which appeal to the *ASL's* need for fun, excitement, challenge and contest. Naturally, other types of students can enjoy and benefit from these materials periodically. Due to the fact that the activities in this center have a high noise factor, it might best be located at the far end of the room away from study stations.

Media Center. If a teacher can acquire the necessary hardware and software to create a media center, it can become an outstanding instructional tool for all types of learners. This area might be located in one corner of the room, and house an overhead projector, a filmstrip machine, a Super 8-mm cartridge viewer, a sound projector, a television, a record player and/or several audio-tape players, all of which can be hooked up to a listening post with headphones in order to keep the noise level down. In this center students can view or listen to commercially produced instructional materials, or materials made by the teacher or other students. Students could also make their own films, tape a story, develop a slide presentation, or work on some other creative task.

Project Center. This would be an area designed for arts and crafts projects and science experiments. The arts and crafts would be particularly appealing to the *ASLs* and the science experiments would appeal to the *CSLs.* This center could provide students the opportunity to construct, invent or do experiments with a chemistry set. Again, all students can benefit in this center depending on the nature of the materials available. It might be best for this center to be located near a sink and water faucet.

Managing The Classroom

The classroom arrangement just described provides a physical environment which will enable the teacher to develop a productive relationship with each student and to guide them in their social and personal development, as well as assist them in learning a specific domain of skill and knowledge. It provides the teacher with the opportunity to become a classroom manager rather than simply a dissiminator of information, and a "staff sergeant" who must keep his subordinates in line.

Appreciation. The most important thing a classroom manager can do is to give students appreciation for what and how they are doing. It can be a great mistake for the teacher to assume that grades are sufficient reward for efforts and accomplishments. All students need appreciation and the amount needed is proportional to what the student accomplishes. Those who accomplish more have a greater need for appreciation than those who accomplish less. As the teacher carries out his role he will have four different opportunities to become aware of the actions and progress of each student and to communicate his appreciation. These opportunities or roles are that of 1) Auditor, 2) Monitor, 3) Instructor, and 4) Assessor.

Auditor. As an auditor the teacher will receive verbal and written reports from students and will listen to or read these reports in order to become aware of what and how students are doing. On becoming aware of these things the teacher has the opporunity to communicate appreciation to each student.

Once students are assigned the task of writing a paper, completing a workbook, or doing some type of individual or group project, the teacher needs to setup times when the students know they are going to report on their progress. As the teacher audits these reports he will also have the opportunity to guide students in selecting topics, developing plans, finding appropriate resource materials, and the like. As he talks with students, the teacher should also be on the look out for any type of strength the students might have. Finding ways to build on strength, to make strength productive, is one of the major challenges of teaching.

Monitor. This provides yet another way for the teacher to become aware of what students are doing and to appreciate their action. Monitoring consists of seeing through first-hand observation the actions of students. By going around the room as students are engaged in an instructional task, the teacher not only can talk with each student, but the student will have the opportunity to show the teacher what he is doing. In response the teacher can give appreciation and encouragement, and of course any needed assistance. The monitoring behavior of the teacher lends considerable support to students as they actually carry out their learning tasks.

Instructor. This role receives the most emphasis in education. Yet, it should only hold equal importance with the other roles. The degree to which instruction is effective is directly related to the degree to which the other roles are fulfilled.

The teacher is not at all different from the coach of a team. A good team can make few achievements under poor coaching. A poor team can make more achievements under effective coaching. It is up to the teacher to design and implement an effective instructional program. As will be illustrated in the following chapters, matching instructional methods, the presentation of subject matter, and the classroom atmosphere to the personality style and learning pattern of students is the key to effective teaching. As students are given a program which is compatible with their way of learning, and they begin to follow directives and take-in information, the teacher needs to reinforce this positive behavior by giving appreciation to students. When the teacher instructs and students follow, this behavior can be encouraged by communicating appreciation.

Assessor. Every teacher is interested in evaluating the level of achievement of students. But this is not enough. Not only does the teacher need to know how students are doing, he also needs to
teacher need to know how students are doing, he also needs to

communicate his apppreciation to students for their efforts and accomplishments. This validating of student effort and progress will have
a reinforcing effect on the students behavior.

Students can also benefit from knowledge of their results. First, it
would be valuable for them to know the extent of their daily achievement. If they are learning math, their papers should be corrected and
returned with a rating of some sort. Second, they should be given some
indication of their improvement aside from their daily score. In the case
of math, this could be done by records on the wall of the classroom or
with a personal chart by which each student could follow his scores.
Third, the students should always know their highest score, for if their
progress begins to decline they can make more definite goals. Knowledge of the highest score is also an incentive for pacing. Fourth, the
students should understand that they can at any time improve faster
than the record shows. Knowing their rate of progress relative to other
students can also be an incentive to many students.

Keeping track of how students are progressing can also be useful
information for determining the effectiveness of the instructional
program. Student achievement can be used as evidence of the degree to
which the educational program is compatible with the learning pattern
of students. For instance, if the *CGLs* as a group are making compari-
tively less progress in a subject than the other types, it may be an
indication that instructional methods or materials are mismatched with
the *CGLs*. Further analysis of the situation could result in the identification of ways to improve the instructional program and the level of
achievement of students.

Gaining Parent Support

Every educator recognizes the value of and the ultimate necessity
for gaining parent support if a program is to be preserved and developed
over time. Typically, parents are interested in what goes on in the
classroom, especially if something different is being done which will
have great *benefit* for their child. The key to gaining their support is
found in the idea of benefit. If parents understand that a program is

going to directly increase their child's interest in school, his willing-ness to learn and his level of achievement, they will be supportive. Each parent knows that what benefits their child benefits them. And, of course, what benefits the student and the parents, will benefit the teacher.

Some might approach parents by inviting them to a large group meeting to tell them about the new program. Though this may seem expedient, it can nevertheless lead to misunderstanding. A more effective approach might be to invite only a few parents at a time to visit the classroom and to show them what is being done. This could be followed by an explanation of the advantages of matching students to tasks and tasks to spaces.

A third approach is to meet individually with each pupil's parents, and begin by discussing their child's learning pattern. This will surely capture their interest. It might be further explained to them that their child has a natural way of approaching tasks, and that he responds best if instruction is matched to his personality style. Most parents will recognize the usefulness of such an understanding, and very likely will want ideas as to how this same understanding can be applied at home. The result of this transaction is that the parents feel good about the teacher and the educational program.

NOTES AND REFERENCES

1. This is a term which refers to a type of space within which the features or objects are moveable so to accommodate the kind of activity that is desired. For a discussion on this type of space, see Edward T. Hall, *The Hidden Dimension*. NY: Anchor Books, 1969, pp. 108-111.

2. This is also a term used to refer to a type of space, but within this space features are fixed and govern the kind of activities that can take place. See Hall, op. cit., pp. 103-107.

3. I first talked about the importance of separating interaction and study tasks and of matching each type of task to an appropriate space in an unpublished paper called "Classroom Proxemics", 1972. Proxemics is a word coined by E.T. Hall and refers to how man's use of space influences his behavior. This idea is fully described in Hall's book, *The Hidden Dimension*, op. cit..

VI

Matching Tasks
To Learners

Learning is inevitable in the normal person. From the time of his birth until his death he learns. The purpose of a formal system of education, is to provide people the opportunity to gain certain skill and knowledge in a manner not possible without planned and systematic effort. However, if the student is going to achieve at his maximum, opportunity alone is not enough. The educator needs to maximize the match between the student as a type of learner and those aspects of the classroom environment which have the most direct effect on his behavior.

The following chapter describes the relationship between each of the four types of learners and two important environmental factors, namely, instructional strategies and curriculum content.

Obviously, implementing these ideas into an instructional program is going to be somewhat complex, and initially it will take more time and effort than teaching all students via the same methods and materials. Faced with having to implement four different instructional programs, the practitioner might be inclined to shake his head and say, "Impossible! I don't have the time to do this," leaving the matching to chance. Yet before one totally rejects the idea, he should pause—is it not better that there be *some* compatibility, however primitive or general this may be? The alternative does not have to be whether there is compatibility or no compatibility, but between different *degrees of compatibility*—how much versus whether.

Instructional Strategies For The ASL

As mentioned previously (Chapter I), instructional strategies are those methods or tactics that the practitioner uses to direct specialized learning processes in the student. These methods will affect the amount of learning that occurs in the student. To the degree that such methods as lectures, demonstrations, discussions, assignments and exercises are compatible with the student's personality and learning pattern, he will grow intellectually.

The *ASL* has been described as having a hunger for action and the freedom to act. He seeks physical involvement; he thrives on competition; he enjoys performing; he loves to entertain and be entertained. If instruction is to be effective, it must draw upon and appeal to this student's abilities and attitudes.

The lecture approach will generally be the most ineffective method to use with the *ASL*. To sit passively and pay attention is not his way. To present this student with detailed factual information or with abstractions is to create a situation that will ultimately result in conflict, for the *ASL* will become disinterested and seek activity of his own choosing. And, this activity will more than likely be disruptive to the class.

If a presentation method is going to be used with this type, it would need to be more like a motivational sales pitch than a lecture. The presentation would need to be dynamic and challenging. If the *ASL* is going to learn from a presentation, he needs variety and entertainment. Audio-Visual aides, for instance, would be beneficial. And, since this type quickly loses interest and is distractable, the presentation should be fairly short.

The content of the presentation will also affect the degree to which the *ASL* will pay attention and learn. If the content has immediate relevance, if it appeals to the *ASL's* interest in risk and adventure, his attention is more likely to be preserved.

This student enjoys talking with others, especially if he is to report on progress. A discussion approach can be effective if it is fast-paced. But, the *ASL* typically will not use a democratic process like the *CGL* does. He instead will tend to respond impulsively and may use this as an opportunity to entertain or perform for the class. A productive discussion requires participants to follow a line of conversation. This does not appeal to the *ASL*. He would rather have a discussion which is leaderless and one that allows for freedom of response.

Action is the key to motivating this student. He needs the freedom to act and to become physically involved. A hands-on experience will satisfy his need for sensation and immediacy. Thus, assignments and exercises will be most appealing to the *ASL*.

Assignments which are compatible with the *ASL* are those calling for him to operate, construct or assemble something. He would enjoy and profit from any assignment which utilized his ability to act expediently and precisely.

Highly structured assignments which require him to set long-range goals, or to do extensive planning, are not likely to be completed. This student needs full control of whatever he undertakes or else he will quickly lose interest. To set goals requires planning, and planning involves shifting one's attention among the possible alternatives. To act deliberately is not the *ASL's* way; to the contrary, the sense of non-deliberateness pervades his learning pattern.

To assign this type a paper-and-pencil task is deadly. To expect him to do workbooks or to read and complete questions on the reading does not match his way of being. Also, assigning him homework is a futile gesture and will provide only an arena of conflict to the student, the teacher and the parents.

The *ASL* has a function lust,and manipulating objects satisfies this longing. Thus placing in his hands materials which he can use attracts him. All types of exercises will be appealing to this student. Especially ones which involve the construction, operation or manipulation of materials or tools. Role playing and dramatization exercises will also be appealing. Instructional games will appeal to his competitive spirit. And, the more game-like a task the better.

Instructional Strategy For The ARL

The *ARL* needs a great deal of structure. He will do best when lessons are presented sequentially in increments that make sense. A lecture approach is effective as long as it is well-organized with the major points being clearly presented. To sit, listen and take notes for a long period of time is done with ease. If this student is presented with an outline to follow he will be most responsive. Also, a repetition of material is preferred.

When the *ARL* is required to be spontaneous and to discuss complex issues he has difficulty. If he is to benefit from a discussion format, he will need to know ahead of time what issues or questions are going to be discussed so he can plan and prepare. He will attempt to do his best as long as he is given directions on how to proceed with a task.

Instructional assignments will appeal to the *ARL*, especially those which call for repetition and drill. For him, such tasks are an end in themselves and will be enjoyed as long as he receives praise for his products. He thrives on clerical tasks. Completing workbooks, programmed learning materials, worksheets and the like will interest him.

This type of student acquires knowledge through diligent searching for facts, frequent review of material, and through reading the textbook and workbook. Commercially prepared materials which are carefully sequenced will be compatible with his learning pattern.

In needing to know exactly what the teacher expects, this student will want highly structured exercises. He will particularly like those exercises which develop his study habits and which require him to memorize subject matter. Socratic questioning by the teacher is also effective with this student. He will not be responsive to role-playing or dramatization, or any type of exercise which requires him to be inventive or spontaneous.

Instructional Strategy For The CSL

The *CSL* is comfortable with a logical, didactic presentation of material. Lectures are effective with this student as long as the material is presented in a concise and coherent manner. If there is a repetition of material he will become impatient and his attention will wander. He is capable of sitting and listening to a lecture for a long period of time and usually will follow-up on the lecture by reading on his own. Since this student usually has many questions, it can be very productive to have a question and answer period either during or following a presentation.

If others are incoherent or have difficulty with complexity, the *CSL* becomes impatient. Thus, a group-discussion method is not typically beneficial for this student. Because he usually will reject the ideas and opinions of those he does not consider to be his intellectual equal, he will prefer to have a discussion with the teacher rather than with his peers.

In being an independent learner, the *CSL* will enjoy assignments that allow him to pursue his inspirations. He will like to seek out information that will answer his many questions. Long-term projects are effective and he will pursue these efforts with little encouragement from the teacher. Such tasks as identifying and studying various kinds of problems, developing theories to explain problems, and putting theory into practice to solve problems match his style quite well.

This type does not have the writing facility of the *CGL*. In fact they tend to dislike written assignments, preferring to put their time into inquiring into problems. They tend to believe that it is a waste of time to communicate to the teacher in writing that they know something.

Assignments which call for the collection and classification of facts and ideas, and which provide the opportunity for inventing, discovering, and designing will be well received. The types of exercises that will be most effective are those involving some type of problem solving or decision making. He will also like brainstorming exercises and seems to enjoy a good debate.

Instructional Strategy For The CGL

An individualized and personalized approach is most effective with the *CGL*. He enjoys interaction and will be enthusiastic as long as there is a personal focus. For instance, when using the lecture method the presentor can preserve the *CGL's* involvement by occasionally making eye contact, or by giving opportunities for comments or questions.

The style of presentation is also important. The *CGL* does not want to be entertained, like the *ASL* does, but rather he wants to be "moved" by the presentation. If the presentor has a monotone voice and displays a flat effect, the *CGL* will become bored and inattentive. But, if the material is presented with enthusiasm, if the presentor is dramatic, and if personal illustrations are used, the *CGL* will be stimulated and motivated. If technical detail is being presented a repetition of material is desirable, since the *CGL* tends to gloss over details.

Because this type enjoys communicating, group discussions will appeal to him. Small group discussions will be preferred over large group discussions since they provide more opportunity for personal interaction.

Assignments which provide the *CGL* the opportunity to be creative and speculative will be better received and more effective than ones involving repetition and drill. This student will prefer writing a play or recording a story on tape more than completing a workbook or filling in answers to questions. He will also like the opportunity to work independently, such as reading a book of his own choosing.

Exercises will be appealing to the *CGL* as long as they provide him the opportunity to interact cooperatively with peers. Competitive interactions have a negative effect on this student since he tends to feel bad for the loser, even when he is the winner. Exercises which utilize the interpretative arts, such as role-playing or dramatization, are effective because they enable him to communicate to others those things that are important to him.

Curriculum Content

As with instructional strategies, each type of learner will show a natural preference for specific curriculum content. It can be expected that the stronger this preference is, the more responsive the student will be to the subject, and the more likely it will be that he will do well in the subject. It is important to keep in mind however that simply because a student has a preference for a specific curriculum content, it does not mean that he will automatically do well in the subject. Some students may not do well because the work is too easy; some, because it is too difficult; others, because they are not receiving the motivation which their personality demands.

As mentioned previously, the *ASL* is the least interested in cultural and intellectual matters. He is typically not concerned with preparing for the future or with storing up wisdom. Instead his interest is in doing. Anything that delays his action holds little interest for him.

When the main curriculum consists in action the *ASL* will do quite well. But when it becomes a matter of preparation, acquiring rules and facts through reading, he becomes disinterested. As the curriculum becomes less active and requires more concentration and attention, he no longer finds the excitement he wants.

The *ASL* typically does not like reading, writing and arithmetic. But he will throw himself wholeheartedly into such activities as instrumental play, musical performance, fine and industrial arts, mechanics, drama and athletics.

To capture this student's interest the curriculum must appeal to his desire for risk, adventure and competition. It must also abound with color and motion. Once this student develops an excited concentration on an activity, he can persevere in that action for hours. As a result, he can develop into an outstanding performer, artist, or adventurer. But if his attention and action cannot be directed, he can become a major classroom problem.

Clerical skill practice is compatible with the *ARL*. Doing arithmetic problems, reading aloud and memorizing spelling words appeal to him. He is interested in learning the factual aspects of science, geography and history. The junior high and high school *ARL* typically gravitates toward business-oriented subjects. He will have little interest in English and literature, and will tend to avoid hard sciences and advanced mathematics. Many have an interest in music, but unlike the *ASL* and *CGL*, they will prefer group performance over individual peformance.

When curriculum consists in studying facts, when it deals with the mechanics of a subject the *ARL* does quite well. On the other hand, if he is required to invent, create or analyze complex ideas he becomes confused and has difficulty. In college this type is attracted to fields of service: business administration, accounting, teaching and nursing.

When the curriculum involves understanding, explaining, predicting and controlling realities it matches the *CSL*. He wants to discover how things and ideas are ordered. He is not interested in focusing on concrete facts, but prefers looking beyond what is present or obvious. He has a curiosity for new ideas, an interest in theory and a taste for complex problems. Finding new solutions to old problems brings enjoyment to him.

To do an impersonal analysis of cause and effect relationships is exciting to these students. They enjoy classifying ideas, applying concepts, designing systems and discovering and learning about the laws of nature. They gravitate toward fields which provide them the opportunity to develop models, explore ideas and build systems. They like science, mathematics, philosophy, architecture and engineering.

The *CGL* wants skill and knowledge which will assist him in becoming a unique identity and which will enable him to have a life of meaning. Learning how to help others is of interest to him. He wants to know how to inspire and persuade others to be more caring and productive.

When the main curriculum consists of recalling facts, learning technical details or studying fundamentals, this student is disinterested. But if it consists of studying human behavior or speculating on future events he will be stimulated and can perform quite well.

The interpretive arts, the arts which involve verbal and written communication match this student's interests and abilities. Studying literature and languages appeals to him. Interest in the affective domain draws him into social studies. He will prefer those subjects that deal with people in a transactional way. He will also enjoy the performing arts and fine arts in that they help him to communicate significant experiences.

VII

The Presentation of Specific Subjects

Many times a student's difficulty in learning a specific subject is not due to something inherently difficult about the subject. Rather, it is in the *manner* in which the subject is presented. If the subject can be presented in a way that utilizes the student's personality and learning pattern, the details of mastering the subject will often take care of themselves.

The importance of subject presentation becomes more obvious if we consider that the degree of one's desire for an activity depends partly on its "meaning," or the belief the person has about the activity. For instance, if a student dislikes reading in class he may not show such dislike when he is able to read a book of his own choosing at home. The most frequent method of changing a student's desire in education is based on this relation to the meaning a subject or activity has to the student. For example, a teacher may try to eliminate a certain behavior by saying that "only quiet students get to leave early"; she may induce the unwilling student to do arithmetic problems by presenting the task as a contest or game. Preferences for doing an activity or for learning a subject matter can be changed by presenting it in a way that appeals to the student.

In cases where the student consistently shows dislike for or refuses to do an activity at school, even though he does not mind doing the activity in another setting, the relation between the meaning of the activity and the desire to do it is not obvious. For this student, engaging him in the particular activity at school has acquired negative meaning. Even so, these old "habits" can be changed if the activity is presented in a way which matches the student's beliefs, values and interests. The approach is not one of changing the student's personality, but one of presenting the activity or the subject in a way which is compatible with the student's way of being.

Consider that experience in all cases entails the perception of an event or thing and an interpretation of it. These experiences and their interpretations develop into a coherent network of beliefs, or "realities" if you will, which the person repetitively uses to interpret the world. As we have seen, people differ in their beliefs, values and feelings about things and events they experience. These differences become clear when we consider the various types of personality. What is common-place to one type of personality can be utterly devastating to a different type. And yet, each type of personality tends to expect that what he feels is what others feel, what he sees is what others see, etc. Failure to understand the differences in what students experience, judge or interpret can have great consequences to the educator. On the other hand, understanding these differences and utilizing this understanding in presenting subjects to students can lead to exceptionally productive results.

An analogy may help to further clarify this point. A teacher is somewhat like a salesperson in that he is trying to get his customer, the student, to buy various products, in this case the product being certain ideas, content or activities. A good salesperson knows that it takes more than a good product to make a sale. It is necessary to convey to the customer the relevance of the product in terms that make sense to the customer. Thus the salesperson knows that he needs to talk in a language that the customer understands.

Now, by presenting a subject in a way which matches the student's values, interests, likes, and learning pattern, the teacher would be "speaking the student's language." Therefore, it is more likely that the student will buy the product. A good salesperson knows that two different people will buy the same product but for different reasons. And it is these differences that must be appealed to if a sale is to be made.

What follows is a discussion of how specific subjects might be presented to each type of learner in order to maximize its acceptance.

Mathematics

Even though math is important and useful many students are not interested in the subject. This is particularly noticeable with elementary and junior high school students. The fact that the beginning courses tend to focus on the mechanics of the subject may partially account for the negative attitude of many students. When the subject is presented as a series of clerical operations and involves a great deal of repitition and drill, it will be appealing to the *ARLs* but not to the other types.

If the *ASL* is going to learn math, instruction will need to be compatible with his desire for spontaneity, excitement and challenge. Some type of instructional game, for example, would have high appeal to this student. This would be especially true if the pay-off for winning in a game is immediate. As unacceptable as it might be to many teachers, this student needs to see that by doing math he is going to get something he wants "now." To require him to prepare, save or plan goes against his nature.

Instructional tasks should also be short and varied. For instance, solitary tasks might be alternated with more active ones, thus creating a balance in the stimulation level. The practical applications of math should be the major focus. Workbook assignments should be kept to a minimum. Having this student use math to solve problems which are relevant to his current circumstances will be most appealing to his realistic outlook.

When instruction involves the memorization of various operations and is organized according to well-structured routine exercises it will be appealing to the *ARL*. This student enjoys and prefers concrete step-by-step instruction. He likes to learn quantitative facts and practice mechanical operations. He sees a practical value in math and feels secure in the fact that the operations are standard and consistent. If he can focus on the elements of the subject and progress from the parts to the whole he will feel most comfortable.

Learning the principles of math will be of interest to the *CSL*. He will want to use these principles in discerning the organization of nature, and to gain the ability to predict and control realities. For this student math is a special case of logic. The older students of this type will want to know mathematical theory and how it can be used to solve various types of problems in the real world.

A comparison between the *ARL* and the *CSL* will help to clarify the perspectives and needs of each type of student. The subject of musical composition will be used in this comparison. In this subject the *ARL* will focus on the elements of composition and will learn the mechanics of writing. He will learn harmonics and overtones, about consonance and dissonance, about the different kinds of intervals between notes, about the various keys in which music can be played, and the minor and major groups of keys. But when the mechanics of all this are studied he is likely to not have any idea of harmony and melody, no conception of musical proportion and beauty.

The *CSL*, on the other hand, will tend to focus on musical form. He will be interested in designing melodies in a succession of chords which are constructed to create a musical architecture which has unity, proportion, musically balanced wholes.

Most would agree that musical composition has little to do with mathematics. However, the above comparison serves to illustrate very clearly the difference between the *ARL* and the *CSL*. They both do have the ability to deal with detail and to focus their attention but, they have a very different style of approaching a task. The *ARL* focuses on elements and mechanical operations, whereas the CSL focuses on form or configurations.

The subject of math will typically hold little interest for the *CGL*. People are important to this person not numbers. Personal relationships are what he seeks, not competency in math. If this subject is going to gain his attention and effort, it will need to be presented in a manner that is compatible with his attitudes and perspectives. For instance, if mathematics could be presented as having a direct relationship to people and how they live it might take on a meaning that would appeal to this student. To study about the struggles and problems of the Arabs that led them to invent a system of notation would interest the *CGL*. He would also be stimulated by learning about the legends that surround the numbers and reasons why the different digits have their particular shape. He would find significance in learning about the philosophy of life behind each mathematical discovery, behind the discovery of "0," behind the process of adding, subtracting, dividing etc. It is this kind of personal focus that will help preserve the *CGL's* attention on a subject he would rather not have to take.

History

In the book, *The Lessons of History*, Will Durant described history as an ". . . industry, an art, and a philosophy—an industry by ferreting out the facts, an art by establishing a meaningful order in the chaos of materials, a philosophy by seeking perspective and enrichment."[1] The study of history can provide people with many different things. It can provide a recounting of the rise and fall of nations and ideas, or a deeper understanding of human nature, or act as a guide in making current judgments and policies, or from its regularities in sequence of events provide the possibility of predicting and controlling future events.

The study of history can provide something of interest for each type of learner. The task of the educator will be to help the learner discover those things of interest that history has to offer. This is no easy task, yet the alternative of teaching all learners as if they have the same interest, desire and learning pattern clearly will be unproductive.

The *ASL* for instance, does not have a desire to learn dates, names and places, lessons of history, or theories of history. If by some chance his focus does turn to history he will be most interested in how people availed themselves of the opportunities of the time, how they were able to survive hardship, overcome obstacles and meet the challenge of crisis. His personality is such that if he is to learn history it must be presented as something which is exciting, an adventure, the solving of problems in crisis and the taking of risks.

This student would be particularly motivated by a military interpretation of history. War is one of the constants of history and the ultimate in competition. A study of the great battles of history and their heroes may indeed excite the *ASL*. He would probably want to know about the adventures, warriors, disciplinarians and rebels, and how these people gained their places as a force in history. Throughout history the hero of action emerged in response to the exaltation of crisis and acquired a position of power not available during normal times. And, as Durant has indicated, "he is not merely an effect. Events take place through him as well as around him; his ideas and decisions enter vitally into the course of history. At times his eloquence, like Churchill's, may be worth a thousand regiments; his foresight in strategy and tactics, like Napoleon's, may win battles and campaigns and establish states."[2] Voltaire's view of history might also appeal to the ASL, for he described history as mainly "a collection of the crimes, follies, and misfortunes"[3] of mankind.

The *ARL* is a natural historian. He is interested in the factual aspects of history, and seeks to know its lessons. He has the facility for learning names, dates, cities and so forth. His natural desire for belonging and for preserving social institutions, customs, traditions and rituals activates and maintains his interest in the subject. However, as with the *ASL* he will not enjoy, nor will he be interested in historical abstractions.

The *CSL* will not be interested in the concrete body of historical facts as much as he will be in the social and political laws and principles which explain these facts. His interest will primarily be in studying history from a philosophical point of view. He will want to discern the patterns of history, and translate these patterns into principles which have application to making future social and political decisions and plans of action. Analyzing various historical problems, designing alternative solutions to those problems, and predicting the possible effects of such solutions had they been imple-mented are the types of tasks this type would enjoy.

The study of history should provide the *CSL* with a means to "see the moment in the light of the past." He would value knowing how geology, geography, biology, human nature, moral codes of culture, religions, economics and the structure of governments influenced the unfolding of history. Due to his interest in science and technology he would undoubt-edly like to know how certain inventions and discoveries evolved out of historical events, and how the intellect of men of genius was an important force in history.

The *CGL* will desire a personal and romantic view of history. He will want to know about the beliefs and attitudes of the people in the various stages of history, and about their struggles and dilemmas, and how these problems affected them personally. For instance, he would be curious about what the good life meant to the ancients, the medieval man, and to man of the Renaissance, and what it means to modern man. He will not be interested in historical events themselves, but in the meaning of the events in relationship to the people of the time, and to himself. As he studies history he will probably project himself into the situations he is studying, and speculate on how he might have felt and reacted. He will search for the significance of historical events and attempt to understand their meaning.

A "humanistic" view of history appeals to this student. Not only will he be concerned with the struggles of the individuals and the cruelties of the battlefields, he will want to know about the goodness to be found in men throughout history. He will want to learn about nobility, the gifts of charity, and how men helped one another. He would be fascinated by the study of great statesmen, philosophers, poets and artists, and about the prophets, like Mohammed, who were able to inspire men to raise the poor and the weak to a place of great power.

Language Arts

Learning the skills of reading, spelling and composition requires repetitive practice, accuracy and precision. It involves learning about the relationship between letters, words, and phrases, and how context influences the meaning of words. Instructing students in these subjects can be a complex task since not all students learn equally well from the same kind of repetitive practice. Nor do they have the same ability for focusing on details and making sharp delineations. They also differ in their ability to comprehend how context influences the meaning of words.

The *ASL* typically shows little interest in learning the fundamentals of language arts, particularly if he is required to learn for the sake of learning or for some future performance. His interest is limited to immediate circumstances. If he does not see the practical value of a subject, if the subject is not presented in a way which directly applies to his present circumstances, he will become inattentive and seek activities of his own choosing.

If the *ASL* does become interested in language arts, his interest will usually center on reading or writing poetry and, fiction and non-fiction stories. He will not be interested in themes that are philosophical or plots that present man metaphysically, like the *CGLs* tend to do. Stories which focus on "life as it really is" are of more interest to him. Hemingway, for instance, wrote novels filled with physical events. His stories are exciting and involve adventure, challenge and risk. Whether it be war, the bull ring, a big-game safari, or an airplane crash he wrote about how man tested his courage in "real life."

The writings of this type tend to show a close relationship with the physical environment. They often show a respect for nature and the animal world. Robert Frost wrote poems with such names as "Blueberries," "Birches," and "The Wood-pile." He wrote about what he could see, hear, and feel.

The *ASL* tends to enjoy reading books which elicit a spontaneous overflow of feelings. They like to read stories which have a hero who is cool, competent, fearless in action, self-assured, self-confident, and sexually charged. The detective novel, for instance, which is dominated by a sensing-type hero who senses his way to solutions by slugging, shooting, and sleeping around with suspects, appeals to the *ASL*.

Learning the mechanics of reading, spelling, and composition appeals to the *ARL*. He enjoys spelling because words are permanent and have a consistent orderliness. When instruction in these subjects involves memorizing facts through repetition and drill, he will perform at his best. In composition, this student will be responsive to learning punctuation, grammar, and sentence structure. But if he is required to invent or create a story or a poem he will have great difficulty. He is quite capable of writing a summary of the plot of a story or recording physical events, but lacks the natural ability to be imaginative in his writing.

The *ARL* needs well-structured tasks which meet with teacher approval. He would enjoy completing worksheets, for example. A phonics approach to reading would be effective. In fact, many of the traditional methods currently being used by teachers are designed to meet the needs of this student.

The study of language will appeal to the *CSL*, especially if it focuses on the study of grammar and syntax rather than clerical skills. This student wants to study English words and know why they happen to be spelled the way they are. Researching the root of a word matches his pattern more than memorizing how a word is spelled. In composition he will want to know how a story is developed and how it is organized. Learning about different styles of writing would interest him. Most would prefer writing a scientific or technical work more than a fictional or dramatic work.

Language Arts will be of particular interest to the *CGL*. This type enjoys the communication process and tends to have a superior ability to speak and write fluently. They generally have an interest in reading and writing poetry, novels, plays, scenarios, or short stories which are about human beings in trasition. Stories which present moral-philoso-phical positions appeal to them. They are drawn to stories which deal with the realm of ethics—What is good? What are man's proper values? What are the right actions for man to take? They enjoy stories which integrate an important theme with a complex plot structure.

This student would enjoy studying why words have their particular meaning, and how folklore and culture have influenced the way words are spelled and used. He would also enjoy learning about the four attributes of literature: Theme—Plot—Characterization—Style. And how theme and style are used in poetry.

NOTES AND REFERENCES

1. Durant, Will and Ariel. *The Lessons of History*. NY: Simmon and Schuster, 1968, pp. 12-13.

2. Durant, op. cit., pp. 34-35

3. Durant, op. cit., pp. 40-41

VIII

Varying The Classroom Climate

In order to establish an atmosphere which is productive for all students, the teacher will need to be able to vary the climate according to the needs of each type of learner. The *ASL* for instance, will need an existential atmosphere, one that allows him to respond to what the moment brings, and one which is pregnant with excitment, fun, and playfulness. The *ARL,* on the other hand, will do best in a friendly, secure, diligent and hardworking atmosphere. As for the *CSL*, he will respond best in an atmosphere of exploration, invention and discovery. The *CGL* will need an atmosphere which is hermonious, personal, and democratic.

The following chapter deals with the problem of how to establish a classroom atmosphere which is compatible with the personality style of each type of learner. It includes a discussion on how to stimulate student cooperation and responsiveness, and how to instill confidence in each student. It futher deals with issues related to the problem of haw to facilitate the social adjustment of students so that they can enjoy discussing, planning, and working together.

For years social psychologists have been studying the effects that various atmospheres can have on the behavior of social groups. One of the original studies, by H. Anderson in 1939, was an analysis of the behavior of kindergarten children and teachers which revealed that the children reacted to an aggressive approach with aggression, and to a friendly approach in a friendly manner.[1] Early studies by Lewin, Lippitt and White (1939),[2] and Lippitt (1940),[3] suggest that when the mood, spirit or tone is hostile, defiant, stifled, factional or filled with a sense of hopelessness, people will tend to act in ways consistent with that atmosphere. Their behavior becomes unproductive. On the other hand, an atmosphere which is friendly, personal, harmonious and filled with a sense of mutual dignity and respect promotes productive work and facilitates the social adjustment of people.

The importance of the issue of atmosphere in education is analogous to the fundamental importance which the field of gravity, the electrical field, or the amount of pressure has for physical events. Whether we are looking at human or physical events, the atmosphere has a strong influence on the nature of those events. Every teacher, knows that the success of teaching any subject depends largely on the type of climate he is able to create.

The Teacher-Student Relationship

It will be the teacher who sets the spirit, tone, or climate of the classroom, and this begins with the type of relationship he establishes and maintains with each type of learner. The teacher-student relationship is to be one based on influence. The teacher is to direct, give and instruct, and the student is to follow, receive and learn. Essentially, the teacher is to control what goes on in the classroom.

Some may think that establishing such a relationship is not a difficult task, particularly since the teacher is in a socially sanctioned role which gives him the authority to influence the student. Also, the educational locale is a designated place in which the student expects to be influenced. The setting is sharply distinguished from the rest of the student's environment by its special qualities, including clearly delineated temporal and spatial boundaries.

And yet, the experienced teacher knows that it takes more than authority and locale to get students to learn, particularly to achieve at their maximum. In the end, it will be the teacher who must establish and maintain a relationship with each student which elicts his cooperation—his willingness to follow directions, receive information, and learn from the teacher. Unless there is cooperation no amount of instruction will be effective.

If the student is to be influenced, he must first perceive the teacher as a person who is benevolent—as someone who cares about his welfare.

The idea of professional caring is not easily described. It means that the teacher gets involved with the student to the extent that it matters to the teacher what happens to the student. Caring in this sense does not necessarily imply approval, but rather, a determination to persist in trying to help no matter how much difficulty the student has in learning. It is the idea that the teacher communicate through his involvement that he cares and that he has the student's best interest in mind. It is not the same type of caring that family members feel toward each other. It is more the type of caring William Glasser describes as simply becoming involved in a way which implies that what happens to the student makes a difference to the teacher.[4]

Being a person who cares does not mean that negative emotions are never to be expressed to the student. Peculiarly, most students will accept a negative response from the teacher if they sense the sincere desire to help behind an openly expressed negative emotion. In fact, the teacher's expression is motivated by the intent to be constructive, the very display of emotion may convince the pupil of the sincerity of the teacher's concern for him.

It is the type of involvement the teacher has with the student that will determine whether the student sees the teacher as someone who is caring. The nature of this involvement will be determined by the teacher's behavior and the student's personality. It will be the student's personality which determines how he will interpret or perceive the teacher and his behavior. Thus the teacher must act in ways that match with or are compatible with the student's perspective.

The significant point is this: To the degree that the teacher responds in ways which are compatible with the student's personality, he will be perceived as benevolent. As he displays to students that he understands their needs for self-esteem, and as he provides them with the opportunity to fulfill those needs, he is showing students that he cares enough to establish and maintain rapport with them.

This willingness to care enough to provide the student with what he needs and with what will be of benefit to him, defines the teacher as a benevolent person. As a result students will be cooperative and an atmosphere begins to emerge which facilitates and enhances the teaching and learning process.

There is another result that occurs from the teacher's involvement and caring—it creates in the student a sense of expectancy. Being convinced that the teacher is interested in him has the effect of mobilizing the student's expectation for success. He feels that since the teacher is an "expert," this means that he understands the needs of students and knows how to help them learn. And certainly, he would not spend so much time and effort unless he believed some benefit would result. Thus, a powerful boost to the student's hope for success occurs.

Balancing Freedom And Restraint

Cooperation with one another has always been the basis of productive social organization, and is the result of a balance between freedom and restraint. Freedom and restraint are not mutually exclusive. They are reciprocals, and both are necessary for order to exist. History, for example, shows us that total freedom has led nations to chaos, while restraint alone has led them to rebellion, but rebellion is eventually tempered by restraint.

Consider the animal. Caught and caged, it never reconciles itself to captivity, and paces about forever on the watch for a way for freedom. Totally free, however, and having all of its needs met, it becomes docile, inactive and only when it meets restraint does its activity increase.

How the teacher handles the problem of freedom and restraint in respect to the four types of learners will influence the kind of classroom atmosphere created and will influence the degree to which each type of learner becomes productive. Many teachers vacillate between imposing restrictions and letting the students determine their own order. Some try to force students to stay within certain boundaries, others let students do what they want to do. Neither approach gets satisfactory results.

Students need restraint. They need guidance and information however, rather than prohibition and commands. They need to learn to submit to knowledge rather than to regimentation. They need to learn to achieve order, not through restriction and compulsion, but through the spread of intelligence.

A classroom which is dominated by the teacher may initially appear to have order, but in such an atmosphere students are more likely to be aggressive against their peers, although submissive to the teacher.[5] If there is too much restraint, students become frustrated, competitive, and aggressive toward one another.

Trouble comes when educational demands are not sufficiently varied from the student's point of view. Personality needs restraints, something from which to rebound, but when restraints become too great, the student begins to have difficulty. Evidence of this basic truth is found in the observation that children who always have their own way, deliberately make trouble to meet with restraint. On the other hand, a person who is constantly restricted rebels and fights for his own initiative.

The ASL *wants* freedom from restraint. He seeks to be spontaneous, to respond to the urge, the impulse. He needs to be active and to have space for moving freely. Yet, with too much freedom, he becomes overstimulated, too active (hyperactive), and his behavior becomes disruptive. Work periods need to be short and varied, and balanced with quiet activities. He could benefit greatly from relaxation training.

This student also has a need for fun and excitement. He enjoys entertaining and being entertained. Without enjoyment he becomes bored, jittery, and engages in random behavior, seeking the needed excitment where ever he can find it. Once assigned a task he needs full control of his own activities, He will lose interest if others interfere, for he wants to discover his own order of doing things. Even though he does not have a natural interest in concentrating, or delaying his impulses, or dealing with complex material, practice in such things is much needed.

The **ARL** *enjoys* structure, routine and ordered. He does not have the same need for variety and flexibility as do the other types of learners. In fact, too much freedom, or constant change and variety, is disruptive to him. He can become anxious if things appear inconsistent, temporary, or chaotic. Too much restriction on the other hand, can be a problem if it inhibits his ability to satisfy his needs for social belonging, and yet he is less affected by restriction than the other types of learners.

The **CSL** *is* a non-conformist and has a strong need for independence. He needs time to explore, investigate and to discover the answers to his many questions. If given too many restraints, particularly restraints he sees as unwarranted or unnecessary, he becomes impatient and may become disrespectful and challenge the teacher's authority. However, if he is allowed to spend all of his time dealing with intellectual matters he will not develop many of the social and interpersonal skills that can serve him well in life. He needs assistance in developing social skills and in learning how to establish realistic priorities and expectations.

The **CGL** *seeks* recognition of his individuality, and his personal worth. He values autonomy and will be extremely sensitive to restrictions, to the notion of authoritarianism, or, to any attempts by the teacher to circumscribe individuality. If his autonomy is threatened he may become negative, resist the teachers authority, and attempt to turn other students against the teacher's efforts. A restricting environment can also cause him to become withdrawn, and to experience feelings of insecurity. At the other extreme, an overly permissive atmosphere can cause him to become discouraged, and create in him the feeling that he is unimportant to the teacher. After all, "If the teacher really cared he would be acting to my benefit and set some standards for me to follow."

Personal involvement is vital to this student, both with the teacher and with peers. He needs the opportunity to participate in creating a pleasant and nourishing classroom environment, and to gain recognition for his emotional attitudes. Finally, since this student tends to be satisfied with a global, diffuse grasp of learning, it would be well to train him to pay attention to details, to obtain more than a general impression of a subject.

Feedback That Motivates

An important condition for efficiency in the learning process is for the student to know how he is doing—he needs feedback on his achievement. Students do not only learn in order to accomplish something or to gain a reward. More often, they learn in order to gain appreciation from others. The receiving of appreciation can be an enduring source of strength for meeting challenges. Without such appreciation even the most productive student can become discouraged.

The **ASL** *needs* feedback on his *performance*. He does not seek praise for his products, or for being competent, or the recognition that he is valued. He wants to know that he has impact on others; that they like and enjoy his performance. This type of feedback will make him feel good about himself and those around him.

He will be responsive to feedback which gives recognition to the clever, quick ways he works, and to his grace and flair. If the task involves risk and taking chances, this should be mentioned. He will be motivated by appreciation which notes his bravery, courage, endurance and timing—for these are all things in which he has pride.

This learner will not be motivated by good grades, or praise for completing a task, or for turning work in on time. He is not interested in learning for its own sake. Learning is a result of his performance. It is a by-product of his action. He is like the actor who learns his lines only so he can perform for the audience. If he is to acquire skill and knowledge, he must have the opportunity to present, demonstrate or perform, and then to receive appreciation for his performance.

The **ARL** *wants* praise for his *products*. He has a desire to please the teacher and will lose interest in a task if his approval is not forthcoming. He values good grades, and will be motivated by such symbols of approval as gold-starred papers, awards, trophies, ribbons and badges. He enjoys the honor of special privileges and duties, and will also value verbal encouragement.

Feedback which validates his desire for caution, carefulness, thoroughness and accuracy will motivate him. To be told that his product meets the set standards is valued. Receiving comments which recognize him as being responsible, loyal, and industrious validates his sense of belonging.

The **CSL** *wants* to be competent, and feels best about himself when he has the sense of being capable. He needs feedback on the *quality* of his achievement, on its coherency and efficiency.

In having high capability hungers, this student soon begins to develop equally high inner standards of improvement. He must meet these standards. Report cards can therefore have a negative effect. Once he achieves high grades he begins to expect that every grade should be high, and if he does not receive top grades he begins to doubt his own ability. At this point he needs a great deal of encouragement, direction on how to improve, and the assurance that he is capable.

The **CGL** *hungers* for a sense of identity and one way he gains that is through *personalized* acknowledgement from the teacher. He needs the assurance that he has worth and importance to those around him. To be recognized as a unique person making unique contributions is his ideal. He will thrive on personal attention. A physical touch or physical closeness motivates him, and he likes to be called by his first name. A personal note on his papers will also serve as a powerful motivator.

Status-Role Assignments

Humans are primarily social beings. That which makes people

distinctly human is a result of their relationship to the social group. Group membership is a necessary part of development. Social striving is primary and the search for a place of status is basic to every child and adult. The role that one plays in the group influences how he perceives himself relative to the other members and influences how he behaves.

When a person selects or is given a role which is accepted, he can have a sense of well-being, and behaves productively. If his role is rejected, he experiences a sense of ill-being and becomes unproductive. The person who plays the role of a helper, friend or caretaker, for example, has the opportunity to gain a sense of respect, importance, belonging or achievement. On the other hand, if he plays the role of persecutor, victim, troublemaker, or martyr he can lose respect, and be rejected by the group.

Many teachers have discovered the value of assigning a student some kind of job in the classroom, like being an assistant or monitor. Whether the student sees the task as a privilege, freedom, duty or responsibility, the fulfillment of such a sanctioned job provides him with a sense of achievement and also gives him status. This can be a powerful motivator for the student.

Carefully watching and guarding a student's status can be immensely helpful to preserving his well-being, cooperativeness and his willingness to deal with the difficult situations that are bound to occur in life. When a person feels good about himself and others, he has more energy and a stronger desire to successfully handle problems of living.

Students do not necessarily have a constant need for a status role. In fact, such roles need only be assigned occasionally. The occasional assignment is like giving the student an inoculation which provides him with psychological antibodies which help to counteract stresses and strains, and preserve his well-being.

There are many roles a teacher can use to provide students with status. For instance, in addition to a classroom monitor or assistant, he could assign the job of classroom nurse, librarian, counselor, receptionist, or historian. Which kind of role to assign a particular type of learner will not only depend on his being able to fulfill the role, it also is contingent on his personality style. What one type of learner perceives as offering him status may not be so perceived by a different type of learner. Being assigned a seat next to the teacher, for example, to one type of learner may clearly provide him a unique place, and his status would be higher than if he had a seat in the back of the room. A different type of learner may perceive this same assignment as a restriction of his freedom and punishment.

The ASL *would* enjoy such roles as the classroom artisan, entertainer, or promotor. He might also like being the official clown, comedian, jester, master of ceremonies, demonstrator of experiments or projectionists. Roles which utilize his desire for performing, acting, operating, and which utilize his interest in risk, challenge and excitement will be well received.

Roles which require being responsible and giving service will appeal to the **ARL**. This student would enjoy being the classroom treasurers, librarian, historian, nurse, janitor, or caretaker. He would like being the accountant, conservator, seller, or administrator.

Such roles as the classroom philosopher, designer, inventor, scientist or president would appeal to the **CSL**. He might also like being the science consultant, math consultant or statistician. Roles which provide him with the privilege to do independent research, or to have time to invent would also be highly appealing to this student.

The CGL *values* personal relationships. He desires to bring out the best in others, and likes to be creative. Such roles as co-teacher, tutor of younger students, classroom counselor, host, receptionist, official correspondent, journalist, author or poet will appeal to this student. He would enjoy either writing, directing or producing a play, or writing an autobiography, diary or the like.

Many kinds of roles can be created by considering that *places* and *things* are of immense value in fixing status. For instance, possessing a certain object, ornament or tool can give a student the sense of status, as can having a special place or space in the classroom.

Times and *sequences* can also create a sense of status. For some students, being the first one to present a paper to the class, or to leave the classroom for a break, can have value. The degree of choice a student has over his activities can also set status.

Status can be set by privileges, freedoms, duties and responsibilities, as well as by things, places, and people. The kind and number of roles any particular teacher has at his disposal for assigning to the different learners is only limited by his own ability to discover such status-givers.

Encouraging The Acceptance Of "Differentness"

Many problems between people occur as a result of a fundamental belief that all people are similar and that any deviation from that similarity goes against the natural order of things.

Visibly we joy in becoming as much alike as possible—in our dress, our hair styles, our possessions, our manners, our morals and our minds. As culture evolves, the acceptance and appreciation of individual differences seems to disappear. The longer we live the more susceptible we become to the opinions of our friends and neighbors; the more imitative and "respectable;" the more attached to custom and convention; the more reconciled to those restraints that create in each of us the idea that we either should be more like others, or that others should be more like ourselves.

Since such forming influences act upon us in our tenderest and most suggestable years, we accept the myth of sameness, in spite of the fact that our experience often informs us otherwise. And, since the differences between people are not difficult to see, in most of us there is triggered a common response: Observing how others differ from us, we conclude that those differences are a result of a flaw or defect and we attempt to correct the error by remaking the person in our own image. We try to change the person's way of thinking and wanting.

As discussed previously (Chapter II), attempts to change *form,* are fruitless. Asking a person to change his personality is like asking a zebra to change his stripes. Form is indelible. To change form is impossible.

The student, then, could profit from becoming aware of and learning to appreciate the different personality styles and learning patterns. Such an understanding would not only help him to have better relationships, it would also help him utilize his own strengths and improve in his areas of weakness.

It would be valuable for students to know what each type of learner brings to the classroom, and how each type typically reacts toward others and what he expects from them.

The **ASL** *brings* fun and laughter to the classroom. He brings a sense that something exciting is about to happen. The atmosphere can become electrified, charged with adventure. His playfulness adds a balance to the work ethic of the *ARL*. He has an eye for the witty and clever, and can be a charming conversationalist, having a repertoire of jokes and stores. He is always ready to spur others into action. Being "cool headed," he can respond to crisis. As a realist he can solve many immediate problems, not being tied to past or future rules or policies.

This student is open-minded and adaptable. He is able to get people to cooperate with each other in the here and now. He has a fraternal outlook and can develop a strong sense of loyalty to his teammates. He is typically flexible and patient, and does not tend to judge his peers. The behavior of others is accepted as a matter of fact. But, at times he may become impatient with the *ARL's* attempts to restrict his behavior, or the *CSL's* focus on abstraction or the *CGL's* focus on becoming self actualized.

The **ARL** *brings* to the classroom his interest in and propensity for preserving social structure, tradition, custom, rules and routines. He has a special sense of social responsibility.

In being "delay-sensitive," this student expects others to make decisions expediently and he does not hesistate to try and correct what he sees as negative in others. He tends to expect others to be stable, reliable and sensible. He tends to misperceive personal transgressions and concludes that "bad acts" mean "bad person." He wants others to earn their keep, and believes that rewards should only be given to the winners, thus not appreciating the lesser achievements of people.

The *ASL* will be perceived as irresponsible and as needing restrictions and controls. He will dislike his impulsive, erratic behavior, but will like his cheerful, personal charm. The *CSL's* desire to change established routines that are ineffective will be resisted, but he will value his insistence on accuracy and detail. He will tend to see the *CGL* as over-emotional, and will dislike his desire for independence, his interest in the novel, his desire for variety and his often dramatic flair. The personal focus of the *CGL*, his caring ways and his ability to make him feel that he belongs, will be appreciated.

The CSL *brings* to the classroom an interest in the sciences and in technical know-how. Discovering ways to increase efficiency and effectiveness of procedures excites him, as does solving complex problems. He displays an enthusiasm for learning which may stimulate the interest of other students.

He will dislike the *ASL*'s disinterest in accumulating knowledge, but will like his boldness, willingness to take a risk, and proficiency in spontaneous action. He will find the *ARL's* parental attitude somewhat irritating, but will value his interest in factual details. The *CGL's* focus on meaning and significance will be viewed as frivolous and somewhat baffling, but his personal warmth and charm will be envied and appreciated.

The CGL *brings* to the classroom a strong interest in and ability to create a warm, human, enjoyable atmosphere. He adds a people-centered point of view. A classroom without this student could become cold, sterile, joyless and dull. This student is capable of activating enthusiasm and a "class spirit." He provides emotional support and social direction to peers. He seeks to create an environment which provides for freedom, autonomy and equality among the individuals.

He will dislike the *ASL's* disinterest in keeping commitments, sharing his feelings and being close. He will also dislike his "anything goes" attitude. He will like this person's easy-going manner, his interest in risk, excitement and enjoying life. He will not like the *ARL's* desire for imposed structure and adherence to tradition, but will find his responsible and stable manner appealing. He will not like the *CSL's* logical and objective manner and his indifference to feelings, but will value his intellectual pursuits.

Summary

It has been stated that willingness to learn, interest in school work, cooperativeness and many other attitudes of the student, must be guaranteed before instruction can be effective. These attitudes depend largely upon the person's responsiveness to the teacher. It is the teacher who must gain influence over the student, and this depends on the kind of relationship he develops with the student. The nature of this relationship will create the climate of the classroom. The teacher-student relationship is among the most potent influences of the classroom, more potent in the long run than the modes of instruction and curriculum content.

If the teacher is able to develop a relationship with the student which is based upon benevolence, the student's cooperation will be elicited and an atmosphere will emerge which is productive to the teaching and learning process. This relationship is established and preserved when the teacher displays to each type of learner that he understands his needs for freedom and restraint, for appreciation and for social status. In this way he is showing each student that he has his benefit in mind and that he cares enough to establish and maintain rapport with him.

NOTES AND REFERENCES

1. Anderson, H. "Domination and social integration in the behavior of kindergartden children and teachers." *Genet. Psychol. Monogr.*, 21, 1939, pp. 287-385.

2. Lewin, K., R. Lippitt, and R.K. White. "Patterns of Aggressive Behavior in Experimental Created Social Climates." *J. of Soc. Psy.*, 10, 1939, pp. 271-299.

3. Lippitt, R. "Studies in Topological and Vector Psychology in an Experimentally Study of

Effects of Democratic and Authoritarian Group Atmospheres." *University of Iowa Studies in Child Welfare,* vol. 16, No. 3. 1940.

4. Glasser, W. *Schools Without Failure.* NY: Harper & Row, 1969.

5. Lewin, loc. cit.

Appendix A

Learning Pattern Assessment

This assessment will assist in determining a student's natural style of learning. If used with adults, it can be self-administered and self-scored. If used with elementary, junior high, or high school students, it should be completed by a teacher, counselor, school psychologist, or any educator who has had the opportunity to observe the student's behavior in the learning situation.

Read each statement carefully and circle the degree to which the statement applies to or describes the student being assessed. A six point rating system is used, with zero being the lowest (least characteristic) and five being the highest (most characteristic). It is important that each statement be rated. If you are uncertain about rating, take time to observe the student further, for there is no time limit on completing the assessment. Feel free to utilize any available written descriptions of the student's learning behavior contained in his records.

LOW HIGH

1. Prefers tasks requiring the operation, construction or manipulation of objects or materials, over ones requiring reading and writing 0 1 2 3 4 5

2. Seeks a routine structure, wants lessons to be clearly spelled out in step-by-step order, and wants to know the teacher's expectations 0 1 2 3 4 5

3. Keeps a sharp focus on technical details, enjoys complex ideas 0 1 2 3 4 5

4. Learns best in face-to-face dialogue, enjoys discussing the content of lessons with a small group of peers 0 1 2 3 4 5

5. Focuses on the immediate, is not interested in the past or future and does not like to plan or prepare 0 1 2 3 4 5

6. Prefers a clearly defined, routine schedule, with little variation from day to day, and diligently follows such a schedule 0 1 2 3 4 5

7. Likes to experiment and invent, enjoys analyzing and solving complex problems 0 1 2 3 4 5

8. Has a vivid imagination and prefers fiction, legend and fantasy over the sensible, factual or realistic 0 1 2 3 4 5

9. Likes competitive interactions more than cooperative ones, and is more responsive to instructional games than lectures or discussions 0 1 2 3 4 5

10. Conforms to the standards and expectations of the teacher, and seeks to do what s/he is "supposed to do" rather than taking independent action 0 1 2 3 4 5

11. Has a stronger interest in intellectual matters than in interacting with others on a social or personal level, or than having fun. . .   0 1 2 3 4 5

12. Enjoys the communication process, and has unusual talent for expressing his/her feelings and thoughts 0 1 2 3 4 5

13. Is more interested in the temporary and expedient than the permanent and the diligent 0 1 2 3 4 5

14. Is quiet and orderly, dutifully follows classroom rules and accepts the teacher's authority without question 0 1 2 3 4 5

15. Wants content and directions to be given only once, becomes impatient with repetition and redundancy, and wants others to use precise language 0 1 2 3 4 5

LOW HIGH

16. Is more people-oriented than thing-oriented, is sensitive to
    others and interacts on a personal level 0 1 2 3 4 5

17. Becomes restless and bored when required to study, prepare or
    concentrate, and dislikes written work. 0 1 2 3 4 5

18. Displays a parental attitude in dealing with peers, and corrects
    them when they do not follow the proper rules and standards . .   0 1 2 3 4 5

19. Is intellectually precautious, tends to reject the ideas and
    opinion of his/her peers, prefering to hear what the teacher has
    to say 0 1 2 3 4 5

20. Is satisfied with a global, diffuse grasp of learning, and is note
    good at mastering details or diligently searching for facts. 0 1 2 3 4 5

21. Acts on the spur of the moment and does not show a concern
    with the consequences of his/her behavior 0 1 2 3 4 5

22. Places high value on good study habits, enjoys completing
    workbooks, and likes recitation and drill 0 1 2 3 4 5

23. Is interested in the abstract, wants to use theories and principles
    to explain facts, rather than simply learn the facts or under-
    standing their meaning 0 1 2 3 4 5

24. Prefers a personalized approach to learning, seeks the recogni-
    tion that s/he is important or values and is sensitive to
    rejection. 0 1 2 3 4 5

25. Responds to classwork only when s/he finds it to be fun and
    entertaining, and becomes inattentive if it requires study and
    concentration. 0 1 2 3 4 5

26. Has difficulty grasping abstractions, does best when learning
    the practical and fundamental aspects of a subject. 0 1 2 3 4 5

27. His/her communicatins are terse, compact and logical, display-
    ing precise grammar and syntax 0 1 2 3 4 5

28. Likes and prefers cooperative interaction, small group discus-
    sion and dramatic play more than competing with peers or doing
    clerical tasks 0 1 2 3 4 5

29. Brings fun and laughter to the classroom, has an eye for the
    witty and clever and likes to tell jokes and stories 0 1 2 3 4 5

30. Enjoys being obligated to others, likes to give service and likes
    to be given responsibility. 0 1 2 3 4 5

                                                                    LOW HIGH

31. Prefers such subjects as science and technology and mathe-
    matics over social studies, history, geography or the arts 0 1 2 3 4 5

32. Is hypersensitive to rejection, conflict, ridicule and sarcasm,
    and empathizes with the hurts and embarrassments of others . .   0 1 2 3 4 5

33. Does not like being confined, wants to be free to roam around
    the classroom and is often disruptive. 0 1 2 3 4 5

34. Enjoys clerical skill practice required in such subjects as arith-
    metic, spelling, reading, and handwriting. 0 1 2 3 4 5

35. Displays a stronger desire to be capable, to gain intelligence,
    than to have freedom to act, social belonging or meaningful
    relationships 0 1 2 3 4 5

36. Is interested in and seems to have superior insight into what
    people think, want and feel 0 1 2 3 4 5

37. Does not like structure, routine or orderliness, prefers to do as
    s/he wishes, and tends to ignore rules 0 1 2 3 4 5

38. Tends to be sensible, stable and practical, and not imaginative,
    creative or ingenious 0 1 2 3 4 5

39. Has a preference for long-term independent projects, which s/he
    carries out with little or no encouragement fromthe teacher . . .   0 1 2 3 4 5

40. Likes and prefers material in the affective domain more than the
    scientific, the mechanical or the historical 0 1 2 3 4 5

SCORING

The assessment produces four scores, which are totals of the four
columns marked A, B, C, D in the score box below. Each score
represents the degree to which the student displays a particular pattern
of behavior. Determine the scores by following the instructions below:

1. Write the points (degree) circled for each statement next to the
   corresponding statement number in the Score Box. For example,
   if you circled a 5 for statement #1, you would write a 5 inside the

rectangle next to the 1 in the Score Box. Be sure to check for accuracy after you have transferred all the points.

2. Add each column and record the total points for each column. None of the totals should be greater than 50 points. Again, check for accuracy: Make sure you have added the columns correctly.

SCORE BOX

	A		B		C		D
1		2		3		4	
5		6		7		8	
9		10		11		12	
13		14		15		16	
17		18		19		20	
21		22		23		24	
25		26		27		28	
29		30		31		32	
33		34		35		36	
37		38		39		40	
Total							

3. Now you have the total number of points for each column. The column having the greatest number of points identifies the student's strongest learning pattern. Each column of the Score Box corresponds to a particular learning pattern:

A = **Actual-Spontaneous Learner**
B = **Actual-Routine Learner**
C = **Conceptual-Specific Learner**
D = **Conceptual-Global Learner**

4. A very clear understanding of a student's learning pattern can be gained by making a visual plot of his learning profile. This is done by plotting his scores using the graph on the next page.

PLOTTING THE PROFILE
COLUMNS

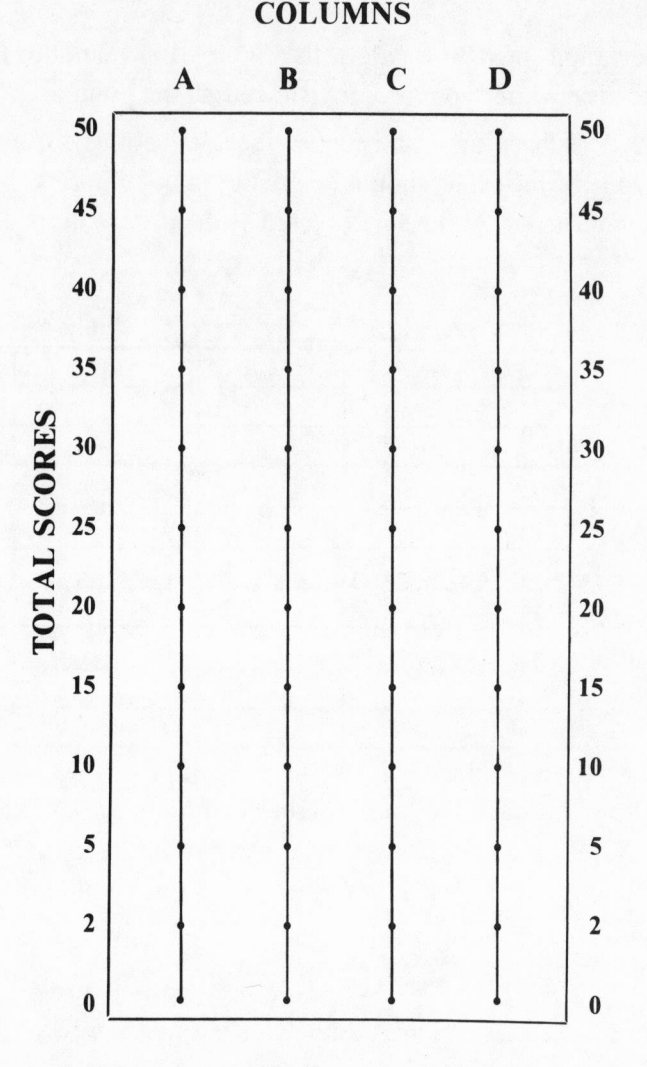

The total scores for each column (A,B,C,D) can be displayed graphically by plotting them on the chart which appears above. The four total scores can be plotted as crosses on the vertical lines on the graph. The four crosses can then be joined by ruling a diagonal line.